T0328406

Teaching International Business: Ethics and Corporate Social Responsibility

Teaching International Business: Ethics and Corporate Social Responsibility has been co-published simultaneously as *Journal of Teaching in International Business*, Volume 11, Number 1, 1999.

Teaching International Business: Ethics and Corporate Social Responsibility

Gopalkrishnan R. Iyer, PhD
Editor

Teaching International Business: Ethics and Corporate Social Responsibility has been co-published simultaneously as *Journal of Teaching in International Business*, Volume 11, Number 1, 1999.

NEW YORK AND LONDON

Teaching International Business: Ethics and Corporate Social Responsibility has been co-published simultaneously as *Journal of Teaching in International Business*, Volume 11, Number 1, 1999.

First published 1999 by Internatonal Business Press®

Published 2021 by Routledge
605 Third Avenue, New York, NY 10017
2 Park Square, Milton Park, Abingdon, Oxon OX14 4RN

First issued in paperback 2021

Routledge is an imprint of the Taylor & Francis Group, an informa business

Publisher's Note
The publisher has gone to great lengths to ensure the quality of this reprint but points out that some imperfections in the original copies may be apparent.

ISBN 13: 978-1-138-99679-3 (pbk)
ISBN 13: 978-0-7890-0832-9 (hbk)
ISBN 13: 978-1-315-86225-5 (ebk)

DOI: 10.4324/9781315862255

Cover design by Thomas J. Mayshock Jr.

Library of Congress Cataloging-in-Publication Data

Teaching international business: ethics and corporate social responsibility/Gopalkrishnan R. Iyer, editor.
        p. cm.
        "Co-published simultaneously as Journal of teaching in international business, volume 11, number 1, 1999."
        Includes bibliographical references and index.
        ISBN 0-7890-0832-7 (alk. paper)
        1. Business ethics–Study and teaching. 2. International business enterprises–Management–Moral and ethical aspects–Study and teaching. 3. International trade–Social aspects–Study and teaching. 4. Social responsibility of business–Study and teaching. 5. Business education. I. Iyer, Gopalkrishnan R.

HF5387.T4 2000
658'.049'0711–dc21   00-021233

Teaching International Business: Ethics and Corporate Social Responsibility

CONTENTS

ABOUT THE EDITOR

Gopalkrishnan "Gopal" Iyer, PhD, is Associate Professor of Marketing at The Florida Atlantic University in Boca Raton, Florida. His recent research in the area of business ethics has been published in the *Journal of Business Ethics* and *Teaching Business Ethics.* Dr. Iyer is a recipient of the Abraham J. Briloff prize for best paper in business ethics. His current research interests include comparative marketing, business ethics, business-to-business marketing and institutional change and economic transition.

Introduction

Gopalkrishnan R. Iyer

The past few years have witnessed a tremendous spurt of interest in business ethics as an academic domain and arena for practical responsibility. This interest and concern for the ethical conduct of individual managers and corporations is only likely to grow further. The dawn of the new millennium will most likely call for increased attention to those fallen by the wayside in the relentless march of economic globalization. The presumed economic logic of globalization lies in the universality of economic principles and business and consumption domains. However, cross-cultural realities and conflicts as well as indigenous perspectives limit the universal application of global principles and challenge the ethical and social responsibility of global players.

Moreover, given that the academic study of both business ethics and international business contain divergent perspectives and domain issues, educators are still in search of the best approaches to integrate ethics and social responsibility issues in the international business curriculum. In terms of pedagogy as well, diverse perspectives and innovative techniques abound, and this special issue is but a mere sampling.

In an overview paper that follows, major perspectives in business ethics as they relate to international business are explored. Fundamental issues and approaches to international business are juxtaposed and some sharp contrasts are noted. These approaches complicate the

---

Gopalkrishnan R. Iyer is Associate Professor of Marketing, Florida Atlantic University.

[Haworth co-indexing entry note]: "Introduction." Iyer, Gopalkrishnan R. Co-published simultaneously in *Journal of Teaching in International Business* (International Business Press, an imprint of The Haworth Press, Inc.) Vol. 11, No. 1, 1999, pp. 1-3; and: *Teaching International Business: Ethics and Corporate Social Responsibility* (ed: Gopalkrishnan R. Iyer) International Business Press, an imprint of The Haworth Press, Inc., 1999, pp. 1-3. Single or multiple copies of this article are available for a fee from The Haworth Document Delivery Service [1-800-342-9678, 9:00 a.m. - 5:00 p.m. (EST). E-mail address: getinfo@haworthpressinc.com].

task of business school professors interested in integrating ethics in international business. Moreover, crucial suspicions are also voiced on the role of the teacher, the ultimate impacts of formal business ethics education, and success of any pedagogical approach.

The tensions between the universal and the particular are reflected in several walks of life and academics. In the case of business ethics and corporate social responsibility as well, such tensions exacerbate the problems encountered by educators. Jones and Lok attempt a bold way out of this "absolutism-relativism impasse" and call for a more grounded approach to understanding capitalism itself. The critique of capitalism, earlier reposed only with those subscribing to alternative views on the control of modes of production, now provides the basis for exploring taken-for-granted issues and generating dialogue, debates, and ultimately, learning on ethics and social responsibility.

Different disciplinary approaches to international business education seek to understand the different domains of international business. However, the ethical issues that are fundamental to each disciplinary perspective are no less resolved in the discipline's domain within international business. LeClair, Clark, Ferrell, Joseph and LeClair offer ethical issues and perspectives from economics, management, finance, accounting, and marketing. These perspectives reflect a broad range of issues within international environment and business functions. The approaches and issues identified in this article should be of immense use to educators teaching foundational international business courses. Moreover, those emphasizing disciplinary aspects of international business from a specific functional discipline can also gain perspectives on the types of issues that emerge in the realm of ethical decision making in other disciplines.

Academic study of business ethics and social responsibility appears most advanced in North America, and several frameworks rooted in the North American individualist ethos have been advanced. What must be particularly relevant, if ethical universalism and ethnocentrism are to be avoided, is the use of diverse perspectives from other regions/cultures in exploring ethical and social responsibility issues in education. Patterson and Patterson, from their vantage point in New Zealand, offer one such perspective. They elaborate and offer insights on *mana* (or, something more than social-power or prestige–the way we understand these) conceived and used within Maori culture. They find tremendous applicability of the concept and use of *mana* to international business and education. One of the obvious links is in fostering community considerations and socially responsible actions. But, subtly, the introduction of alternative perspectives rooted in diverse cultures breaks through and, possibly, discounts emphasis on ethical imperialist stances.

Experiential learning is of particular importance to inculcate an understanding of a wide array of ethical and social responsibility issues. Herremans and Murch offer one such perspective based on their own experience. Ethical values, real-world issues and business activities are intertwined to offer students an understanding of the dimensions, interactions and implication of ethical and socially responsible behaviors. Such creative, action-learning techniques should go a long way in gripping the students' interests, while imparting relevant education.

Approaches to Ethics in International Business Education

Gopalkrishnan R. Iyer

SUMMARY. This paper provides a brief overview of the major issues in international business ethics and issues that should be addressed when incorporating ethics in international business education. Some general pedagogical perspectives and approaches are presented for the integration of ethics in international business courses. *[Article copies available for a fee from The Haworth Document Delivery Service: 1-800-342-9678. E-mail address: getinfo@haworthpressinc.com <Website: http://www.haworthpressinc.com>]*

KEYWORDS. Business Ethics, international business education, global ethics, teaching ethics

I see no property, analogous to "truth," that belongs or does not belong to an ethical judgment. This, it must be admitted, puts ethics in a different category from science.

–Bertrand Russell
Reply to Criticisms

But what greater temptation than to appear a missionary, a prophet, an ambassador from heaven? Who would not encounter many dangers and difficulties, in order to attain so sublime a character?

–David Hume
Of Miracles

Gopalkrishnan R. Iyer is Associate Professor, Department of Marketing, Florida Atlantic University, Boca Raton, FL 33431 (E-Mail: giyer@fau.edu).

[Haworth co-indexing entry note]: "Approaches to Ethics in International Business Education." Iyer, Gopalkrishnan R. Co-published simultaneously in *Journal of Teaching in International Business* (International Business Press, an imprint of The Haworth Press, Inc.) Vol. 11, No. 1, 1999, pp. 5-20; and: *Teaching International Business: Ethics and Corporate Social Responsibility* (ed: Gopalkrishnan R. Iyer), International Business Press, an imprint of The Haworth Press, Inc., 1999, pp. 5-20. Single or multiple copies of this article are available for a fee from The Haworth Document Delivery Service [1-800-342-9678, 9:00 a.m. - 5:00 p.m. (EST). E-mail address: getinfo@haworthpressinc.com].

Over the last several years, the topic of business ethics has witnessed a geometric growth in interest among academics, practitioners, philosophers, and concerned publics. Academic interest in the topic in the U.S., however recent, has advanced to the stage where more academics are now concerned with business ethics as an area of research and teaching. Indeed, almost all business functional disciplines are cognizant of ethical issues and most introductory and advanced business texts published in the U.S. now include ethical issues either as a separate module or integrate such issues within the text. However, despite the proliferation of academic thought and publications on crucial issues of business ethics, there are still debates on the pedagogical aspects of business ethics. Frameworks on the integration of ethics into the business curriculum, even where offered, suffer from lack of cogency, completeness, or convincing argumentation. Moreover, pedagogical approaches are still undergoing innovation, with suggestions and prescriptions outnumbering successful implementation.

Given these and other problems within the area of business ethics, it may appear rather premature to be tackling such issues within international business disciplines, especially given the fact that international business is still grappling with some fundamental domain issues (Toyne and Nigh 1997, 1998). But, at the same time, the reality in international business is characterized by events and forces that call for more immediate attention to business ethics. Some such events and forces in the world economy are: (i) rapid globalization and its impact on global distributions of wealth, power, equality, and poverty; (ii) the growing power of transnational corporations (TNCs); (iii) several emerging markets with lack of attention to basic business principles and systems; (iv) rising ethnic strifes and conflicts, some of which are due directly or indirectly to economic distributions and redistributions, and; (v) the decline in the power and centrality of the nation-state. When compounded with issues from international business practice, such as bribery, corruption, work-related discrimination, human rights violations, marketing of dangerous products, culpability in international human and ecological disasters, political interference in host country activities, etc., one conclusion appears inevitable: *ethical behavior in international business is our strongest hope especially at a time when alternative systems of governing individual and corporate behaviors are at their weakest levels.* Moreover, approaches to conceptualizing ethics in international business are more recent as compared to the broader domain of business ethics, and it can only be expected that such perspectives will grow in number and strength over the coming years.

This paper revisits some of the major issues in international business ethics and provides an overview of issues that should be addressed when incorporating ethics in international business education. The paper is intended to be a broad overview of some major pedagogical issues. Specific ethical issues of relevance to disciplinary approaches to international business are not addressed here. It is hoped that readers would be able extract applications to their specific international business discipline.

ETHICS AND INTERNATIONAL BUSINESS

The fact that national environments of business exhibit remarkable diversity along economic, political, legal, and socio-cultural dimensions is at once, a problem of market opportunity as well as one of ethical conduct. Relative levels of economic and market development, the nature and extent of political and legal factors affecting business, and the differences in the socio-cultural impacts on markets and business, while contributing to the emergence of business opportunities, are also areas where cross-national conflicts in business conduct are bound to occur.

However, it is tempting to simply evaluate and identify international business strategy as one of taking advantage of such market opportunities, while at the same time, minimizing the market constraints. For example, real differences in wages across national boundaries may make the costs of production cheaper in a foreign country as contrasted to one's own; however, it is also possible that overall labor and operation costs are cheaper mainly because of the relative absence or weakness of foreign laws mandating minimum safety standards, insurance and health benefits, and work conditions. A purely economic viewpoint would find no ethical issues here–after all, so long as foreign laws are adhered, a multinational corporation is simply a passive agency taking advantage of differences in operational costs. From an ethical perspective, however, the broader issues are the disparities in operations as well as the differences in work conditions in different national divisions of the multinational corporation. Is a multinational corporation justified in providing lower than usual employee safety, insurance and health in one of its divisions as compared with others?

Ethical issues may also emerge from the clash of business cultures. It is clear that business principles differ across countries and these differences often translate into fundamental differences in employee selection and hiring procedures, conduct of business negotiations, information provided to consumers, pursuit of the self-interest motive, to name but a few. Such cross-cultural conflicts challenge the ethical foundations of multinational business and extant approaches to resolution are only partially satisfactory. Two such approaches are *cultural relativism* and *ethical imperialism.*

For the cultural relativist, ethical issues arise and get resolved within the local context. Apparent cultural conflicts are easy to resolve since the conflict resolution approaches are themselves rooted in the culture in which they emerge. At the same time, there is a resistance to conflict resolution approaches from the outside, since these may not be informed of the local context. For example, if it is commonplace to offer a 10% cut in the value of the goods imported to customs officials in the Republic of Corruption, the cultural relativist finds no moral transgressions in simply conforming to local "cultural" dictates. Indeed, businesspeople may offer the justification of unethical conduct simply on the bases that: (i) such conduct is culturally acceptable and commonplace and/or (ii) the fact that non-conformity to the cultural norm may lead to unprofitable economic consequences.

However, there are several problems with the cultural relativist position. First, is the argument offered by Donaldson (1996): "Cultural relativism is morally blind. There are fundamental values that cross cultures, and companies must uphold them" (p. 49). This argument counters cultural relativism through the existence of supra-national ethical norms and values. Second, if the cultural relativists' credo, "When in Rome, do as the Romans do," holds, then every aspect of business must be evaluated along the same principle. For example, if the host country cultural norms enjoin business to be more socially and community conscious and de-emphasize pursuit of individual gains, such societal rules must be adhered to by the cultural relativist. Unfortunately, that does not appear to be the case: the cultural relativists position appears to surface only in the case of norms that have a potentially positive consequence to business. Third, the cultural relativist position involves a careful identification of cultural norms and rules and subscribing to the dominant norms and rules. However, the dominant norms and rules within a society may have emerged through non-democratic means or through some power principle. The distribution of power may be such that powerful groups may be oppressing other groups within their society (Steinmann and Scherer 1997). The cultural relativist, having forsaken the right to reflect and criticize, simply assimilates with the current power structure. The moral ignorance and lapses of such a position, in say, dealing in South Africa of even a decade ago, can be readily apprehended.

At the other end of the spectrum in the nexus of ethics and international business is the ethical imperialist position, which entreats managers to apply the same set of ethical principles and rules abroad as they would at home (Donaldson 1996). Donaldson (1996) argues that the foundation for this position is absolutism, i.e., there are moral principles that are equally valid and applicable anywhere in the world. Such principles are based on the notion that: (i) there is a single list of moral truths; (ii) such truths are expressed only with one set of concepts; and, (iii) behavior that follows such truths is independent of the context (Donaldson 1996). The ethical imperialist position releases cognitive stress in identifying cultural- and context-specific truths and realities and offers an easy and immediate resolution to any cross-cultural or moral dilemmas. However, the extension of one's own moral principles and values across the borders presupposes that one's own moral values emerge from: (i) higher precepts and are hence, superior and capable of universal application; (ii) successful fair resolutions of alternative perspectives within one's own culture; and, (iii) realization and understanding of the one real truth. It is not difficult to counter the ethical imperialist position, though history is replete with examples of the operation of such principles. For example, theocracy and blind faith have, through history, entreated true believers to uphold their beliefs, even by the sword, against those of "pagans" and disbelievers. Also, it is inconceivable if colonial expansion in the second half of this millennium would have been possible without such beliefs permeating even those otherwise given to reason.

Despite the critique of the two perspectives in and of themselves, some scholars argue for an in-between position, i.e., the recognition that some moral principles should be universal, while in other cases, the context may provide moral answers and justifications (Donaldson 1996). Thus, Donaldson (1989, 1996) advances the argument that fundamental human rights are valid everywhere and that business should not affect such rights adversely. On the other hand, in evaluating issues that do not involve human rights issues, the context should play a part in deciding what is right and what is wrong.

The careful delimiting of the cultural relativist and ethical imperialist positions is intuitively appealing; however, the presumed supremacy of both moral truths and cultural norms, albeit in different domains, is beset with problems of its own. Note, for instance, which moral truths should be considered universal. Donaldson (1989, 1992, 1996) holds human rights to be universally valid and applicable. In principle, it is not difficult to accept this argument; however, in practice the issues become the identification of specific rights, supremacy of individual rights over collective rights, and the recognition and inclusion of diverse perspectives in the elaboration of such rights. For example, the issue of human rights is itself a thorny issue in current business and diplomatic relations between the West and the East Asian countries. While the West holds the Universal Declaration of Human Rights (1948) listing of human rights to be basic and universal, East Asian nations have recently countered that such rights are Western in origin and scope and are inconsistent with "Asian Values" and thus, inapplicable in their countries (see Bell 1996; Jones 1996; Moody 1996; Perry 1997; Sen 1997; Steidlmeier 1997 for more elaborate discussions).

Human rights debates between the East and the West are only one evidence that the space between the cultural relativist and ethical imperialist position may not be free of tensions. Part of the reason is that the two systems of cultural relativism and ethical imperialism counter each other–critique of cultural relativism is based on presumed universality of some ethical values, while critique of ethical imperialism is based on the presumed importance of some cultural values. This debate between the universality of ethics and importance of culture is far from resolution and only some approaches to carefully negotiate an in-between position can be suggested, as attempted by courageous philosophers, such as Donaldson (1996).

In terms of teaching ethics, however, this debate as well as others pertaining to differences in capitalist systems, relative emphasis on profit motives, importance of the individual in relation to the community, etc., have important ramifications on course content as well as pedagogical approaches adopted. If both the cultural relativist and ethical imperialist positions have to be avoided, then moral rules must emerge from the specific context itself, albeit circumscribed by second-order considerations of diversity, fairness and justice principles as they relate to the context, which themselves are outlined from a first-order discussion of these principles.

APPROACHES TO INTERNATIONAL BUSINESS ETHICS

Apart from the broad areas in the nexus of business ethics and international business elaborated above, there are other approaches to business ethics that require consideration in international business as well. These are discussed briefly below.

Alternative Ways of Thinking about Morality

Goodpaster (1985) identifies three forms that could be taken by ethical inquiry: descriptive, normative and analytical. Descriptive (or empirical) approaches to ethics outline the reality in terms of ethical issues and ethical perceptions and focus on the differences between individuals, corporations, and even societies. Stated differently, descriptive approaches focus on the "is" in economic affairs (Donaldson and Dunfee 1994).

Normative (or prescriptive) approaches, by contrast, focus on "ought" in moral affairs (Donaldson and Dunfee 1994). These approaches hold that "good" ethics can be distinguished from "bad" ethics and that moral rights and moral wrongs can be deduced through thought and logic.

Analytical approaches alternate between the identification of moral rules and the application of such rules. As such, they are different from the development of moral rules without an empirical context, as in normative ethics, or the mere observation of moral rules and context without an ethical position, as in descriptive ethics.

Normative and analytical approaches are favored by philosophers, while descriptive methods are favored by business ethicists within specific disciplines. The distinctions in these methods of thinking about morality brings into question, the issue of integration. However, Donaldson (1994) argues that the prospect of such integration at the level of fundamental theory or methodology, however tempting, must be resisted since the logic of prescription differs from the logic of description. At best, the two approaches can be integrated only in some "symbiotic link" that requires "the cooperation of both empirical and normative research in rendering ultimate value judgments" (Donaldson and Dunfee 1994; p. 254).

The normative-descriptive distinction has clear impacts on ethics within the specific international business disciplines. Normative approaches to ethics within specific disciplines may appear to be "grand narratives," attempting universal and generalized ethical principles that may fit specific situations only imperfectly (Robin and Reidenbach 1993). Moreover, given the absence of a unified concept of morality, there can only be different traditions of moral thought. When applied to specific contexts, such differences merely present a diverse array of normative principles, which used to the fullest extent, may often lead to absurd evaluations of any action as ethically correct (Iyer 1997).

In terms of teaching, normative approaches could be used only to identify varieties of moral thinking and possibly providing alternative frameworks which could be extended, modified and adapted. However, it must be noted that the assumed primacy of theory in these approaches is not derived from empirical content and as such, these approaches are impartial even to the context to which they are applied (Iyer 1997). Moreover, any moral theory can be rejected by demonstrating some potentially ridiculous results, while a favored theory can be advanced by showing that it harmonizes judgments in a variety of cases (Murray 1993).

On the other hand, descriptive approaches can be used only to sensitize students to the varieties of issues that could be subjected to moral evaluation and possibly providing students with specific instances that call for further deliberation and elaboration. Again, it must be noted that such descriptive approaches could do more harm than good through a variety of ways. First, the identification of some practice as common could yield confusion of the ethics-free identification of that practice with business principles. Mere prevalence of a practice may detract attention away from the moral evaluation of the practice. Second, even if a prevalent practice is identified as unethical, it may be assumed that ethical violations are less severe and hence, possibly, have less severe consequences. Third, prevalent practices may be mistakenly elevated to the status of cultural traditions and norms. For example, in the case of bribery, some scholars and practitioners alike have erroneously made cultural generalizations from a prevalent practice, such as: "bribes are an acceptable business custom in the Republic of Corruption." Finally, a cultural relativist position may emerge, which, of course, would be unacceptable given the critique offered in the previous section.

Philosophy versus Practice

Closely related to the normative-descriptive debate, is the question of ethics-as-philosophy versus ethics-as-practice. The former view enables a somewhat objective position to the question of ethics, while the latter is grounded in offering ways of action under specific contexts. The latter method is favored by business ethicists, who argue that unless ethics can be guides to action, they remain merely context-free, abstract and inapplicable to the decision-making context at hand.

The issue of philosophy versus practice has important implications for the role of the teacher/trainer. For example, Klein (1998) argues that "it takes a specific expertise to teach ethics, of which business ethics is a subset, and such expertise, like all expertise, is not something possessed by just anyone." Such a conclusion is valid, if the content of business ethics is ethical theory, for it cannot be expected that business school professors may have the necessary philosophy background to be aware of ethical theory and theorizing. On the other hand, philosophers cannot be expected to have disciplinary expertise and the complete grasp of practical exigencies for ethical issues as they emerge within specific disciplines and business functional areas.

The question of ethical content is also important. To be sure, if ethics is integrated in the curriculum as a prerequisite, core or elective course on ethical theory, it is best left with philosophy professors. However, if ethics is to be integrated within each discipline, it can only be appropriated by those charged with teaching the specific discipline.

Perhaps what appears relevant is a suggestion offered by Goodpaster and Mathews (1982): business executives should be more philosophical and moral philosophers should be more practical. In terms of gaining appropriate content and methods for the integration of ethics, interdisciplinary and cross-disciplinary exchanges between and across the business disciplines and philosophers (as well as sociologists and anthropologists) appears to be a necessary first step.

The Ethical Agent

Business ethics also offers differing perspectives on the primary moral agent. Is the individual manager responsible for moral decisions and actions, or should moral agency be with the corporation? Individualist conceptions of business ethics are the dominant framework in North America, rooted as it is in according primacy to the individual as well as to law and formal rules (Badaracco 1992; Vogel 1993). On the other hand, European and Japanese approaches to business ethics emphasize collective and shared understandings of the community as well as on corporate responsibilities (Takahashi 1997; van Luijk 1990). Given that the extra-individual context and forces can only offer guides to ethical action, it could be argued that the ultimate responsibility for ethical decisions and actions lie with the individual. But, on the other hand, the exoneration of individual responsibility may also emerge, i.e., individual failure in acting ethically may be attributed to "rational" individual pressures, such as threats to career advancement and well-being, authority of superiors, and socio-cultural influences (Iyer 1999).

The corporation-as-a-moral agent is the dominant perspective, especially within international business. The organizational forms and activities of the multinational enterprise (MNE) have been subjected to ethical analysis in recent times (DeGeorge 1993; Donaldson 1989, 1996; Rogers, Ogbuehi and Kochunny 1995; Steinmann and Scherer 1997). However, perspectives differ on exactly how much responsibility is vested with the corporation. For example, Donaldson (1989) argues that given the narrow mission of the profit-making MNE, the MNE cannot be held accountable for a variety of moral aims, including that of distributive justice that enhances general welfare. Thus, Donaldson (1989) identifies realms of minimal and maximal duties for the MNE and holds MNEs responsible for upholding basic international rights and ensuring that these are not deprived by MNE operations. On the other hand, the MNE is absolved of responsibility to correct rights already violated or aid those deprived of such rights irrespective of MNE operations (Donaldson 1989).

DeGeorge (1993) contends that MNEs should not only avoid harmful activities, but also strive to do more good than harm. But, others, such as Velasquez (1995) and Iyer (1998), offer more stringent responsibilities for the MNE that go beyond basic moral rights and include considerations of justice and equality.

It is clear that the economic objectives of the MNE may conflict sharply with the political objectives and socio-cultural environments of nations in which they do business. The sharp divergence of economic principles and ethical precepts can be made readily apparent to students in some instances, such as bribery or manipulation of host governments; however, in other instances, the corporation-as-a-moral agent is not a perspective that can be readily understood in a classroom. Students may be best able to grasp ethical issues and identify ethical courses of actions for themselves, but they can only conceptualize such issues and actions for the case of the corporation. It is not that corporate morality is a subject matter for the real world; it is simply a question of elaborating all details on the extent of individual decisions and actions on corporate affairs, as well as the perspectives of all stakeholders to the business. Such perspectives are useful in entrepreneurship courses, where the student is to be a future business owner rather than a future business manager.

Ethical perspectives in international business also identify international agencies and their formulations of codes of appropriate business conduct. Such code-based approaches are attractive in that they add some "universal" elements to discussions on ethical issues; on the other hand, from the perspective of the reality of international business, it is debatable whether such codes are assured universal application, adherence and governance (Iyer 1999).

Ethical Decision Making

Ethical decision making could be viewed similar to any rational decision making and as such, could follow similar processes (Jones 1991; Rest 1986). To illustrate, Rest (1986) conceptualizes ethical decision making as following a four-step process: (i) recognizing moral issues; (ii) making moral judgments; (iii) establishing moral intent; and, (iv) implementing moral actions. Jones (1991) elaborates this model by identifying moral intensity (i.e., the imperative to make a moral decision) as a crucial driver of the extent to which moral decisions will be made on a specific issue.

Such frameworks of ethical decision-making complement other general decision-making frameworks in formal education. However, the general applicability of the decision structure provides little guide to the decision itself; it remains uninformed by ethical content and considerations of morality. But, nevertheless, the structure resembles rational decision making processes as those that students are entreated to follow when analyzing business cases and such frameworks may be useful guides to offering recommendations therein.

ON TEACHING BUSINESS ETHICS

Apart from the diversity of issues in international business ethics education, further complexity is added when attempting to grapple with the right method of instruction. It should be clear that the right method is guided in turn, by the objectives as regards ethics education. Here, the limitations of formal education must be noted.

It must be recognized that classroom approaches are devoid of the real-life pressures and considerations, such as impacts of decisions on career advancement and family stress, acceptance by peers and superiors, impact on profitability, and stakeholder interests, to name but a few. Hence, it cannot be expected that even if students get their morals right in the classroom, they would do so in the real-world. But, a dissension to this can also be noted in that it may be equally unrealistic to presume that good students (as measured by GPA) would also turn out to be good managers. Similar problems of false positives must be noted in ethics as in business education.

Further, the fact that there cannot be universally-valid rights and wrongs underscores the evaluation of ethical training. Absent scientific basis, such as in pure sciences or mathematics, ethical responses can only be evaluated through: (i) correct application of a given moral principle; (ii) justification of a moral recommendation; and, (iii) the ability of the moral recommendation to achieve a Rawls-ian *overlapping consensus* among disparate perspectives and values.

Finally, the success of any technique adopted can be less noted through its operation in the real world. Take for instance, the role of formal business education in the success of individuals in corporations. Indeed, career advancement of individual students can be tracked and some individuals may even credit their business schools for their career success through public statements and generous endowments. However, virtuous behaviors may not be so readily recognized and, if the assertion that unethical behaviors in the real-world often goes undetected and unpunished (Bhide and Stevenson 1990) is valid, then our future ethical managers are to be found more in the bottom-rungs of the organizational ladder.

A full account of the sheer diversity and innovations in techniques for imparting business ethics education and a detailed evaluation of each technique would take a separate volume by itself. But suffice it to say that the relevance of the techniques and their success depend to a large extent on the objectives of the course and the instructor. If the objective is merely to sensitize students to ethical issues, several innovative techniques could be used. One is through identification of ethical issues within any business functional case. Here, even if the case is on a specific business topic (and less to do with ethics), an ethical perspective could emerge. For example, in a case on multinational entry strategy, students could be forced to reflect on the ethical impacts of such entry and how their recommendations would differ if ethical principles were to be included as criteria in decision making.

Identification of ethical issues and cross-cultural diversity could be obtained also through literature (Shepard, Goldsby and Gerde 1997); videos, films and dramas (Berger and Pratt 1998; Graventa 1998; Hosmer 1997); and, collaborative learning approaches, such as team work and discussion, role plays, etc. Moreover, such approaches may also help uncover specific cross-cultural ethical issues and identification of divergent perspectives to ethical dilemmas.

The objectives of ethical decision-making could be imparted through traditional as well as non-traditional case methods. Here, the focus is clearly on forcing students to think through various issues and make decisions that reflect ethical priorities.

The disparities between formal ethical education and business practice could be bridged, albeit partially, through guest lectures by business practitioners. Specifically, the "guests" could be called upon to relate instances of what they considered were major ethical dilemmas and offer perspectives on how they were guided in taking ethical decisions.

However, whichever method is adopted, it should be clear that perspectives and resolutions of ethical dilemmas should be cognizant of the pitfalls of ethical imperialism, cultural relativism, ethnocentrism, and a pure self-interest maximization perspective.

CONCLUSION

While international business theory, practice and education are only beginning to take stock of ethical issues, perspectives on ethics as well as its pedagogy already exhibit a remarkable diversity of positions, issues, and methods. Given the primary economic nature of globalization as well as the growing opposing currents of ethnic identities, it is only expected that cross-cultural conflicts will increasingly call for greater attention to issues of ethics, notably, diversity, fairness, and justice. While the debate is still ongoing on the moral responsibility of the multinational corporation as well as on the nature and scope of ethics in international business, the lack of resolution of key debates must not lead to inertia when it comes to incorporating ethics in international business education.

Perhaps descriptive approaches may provide a better starting point in international business ethics education, since these approaches may at least achieve the core objectives of identifying ethical issues in a cross-cultural business context. However, it is imperative also to focus on normative aspects of ethics, so that the tools and frameworks necessary for ethical evaluation are provided to the first generation of students, while honing these approaches to reality for later generations. The challenges of integrating ethics in education are many and varied, and it is hoped that in the coming years, business school professors will meet these challenges head-on with concerted efforts in developing methods for realizing a future of ethical managers and responsible corporations.

REFERENCES

Badaracco, Jr., J.L. (1992), "Business Ethics: Four Spheres of Executive Responsibility," *California Management Review*, 34(Spring), 64-79.

Bell, D.A. (1996), "The East Asian Challenge to Human Rights: Reflections on an East West Dialogue," *Human Rights Quarterly*, 18 (August), 641-667.

Berger, J. and C.B. Pratt (1998), "Teaching Business-Communication Ethics with Controversial Films," *Journal of Business Ethics*, 17 (December), 1817-1823.

Bhide, A. and H.H. Stevenson (1990), "Why Be Honest if Honesty Doesn't Pay?" *Harvard Business Review*, 68 (September-October), 121-129.

De George, R.T. (1993), *Competing with Integrity in International Business* (New York: Oxford University Press).

Donaldson, T. (1989), *The Ethics of International Business*, (New York: Oxford University Press).

Donaldson, T. (1992), "Can Multinationals Stage A Universal Morality Play," *Business and Society Review*, 81 (Spring), 51-55.

Donaldson, T. (1994), "When Integration Fails: The Logic of Prescription and Description in Business Ethics," *Business Ethics Quarterly*, 4(2), 157-169.

Donaldson, T. (1996), "Values in Tension: Ethics Away From Home," *Harvard Business Review*, 74(5), 48-62.

Donaldson, T. and T. W. Dunfee (1994), "Toward A Unified Conception of Business Ethics: Integrative Social Contracts Theory," *Academy of Management Review*, 19(2), 252-284.

Garaventa, E. (1998), "Drama: A Tool for Teaching Business Ethics," *Business Ethics*, 8(3), 535-545.

Goodpaster, K.E. (1985), "Toward An Integrated Approach to Business Ethics," *Thought*, 60(237), 161-180.

Goodpaster, K.E. and J.B. Mathews, Jr. (1982), "Can a Corporation Have a Conscience," *Harvard Business Review*, 60 (January-February), 132-141.

Hosmer, L.T. (1997), "Video Review: A Question of Power: Hydor-Quebec and the Great Whale Controversy," *Teaching Business Ethics*, 1(1), 97-106.

Iyer, G. (1997), "Integrating Business Ethics in Classroom Teaching: Some Preliminary Considerations," *Teaching Business Ethics*, 1(3), 315-331.

Iyer, G. (1998), "Ethical Issues in International Marketing," in B.N. Kumar and H. Steinmann (eds.), *Ethics in International Management*, (Berlin: Walter de Gruyter), pp. 221-241.

Iyer, G. (1999), "International Exchanges as the Basis for Conceptualizing Ethics in International Business," *Working Paper*, Department of Marketing, Florida Atlantic University, Boca Raton.

Jones, S. (1996), "Asian Human Rights, Economic Growth, and United States Policy," *Current History*, December, 419-427.

Jones, T.M. (1991), "Ethical Decision Making by Individuals in Organizations: An Issue-Contingent Model," *Academy of Management Review*, 16(2), 366-395.

Klein, E.R. (1998), "The One Necessary Condition for a Successful Business Ethics Course: The Teacher Must Be a Philosopher," *Business Ethics Quarterly*, 8(3), 561-574.

Moody, Jr., P.R. (1996), "Asian Values," *Journal of International Affairs*, 50(1), 166-192.

Murray, T.H. (1993), "Moral Reasoning in Social Context," *Journal of Social Issues*, 49(2), 185-200.

Perry, M.J. (1997), "Are Human Rights Universal? The Relativist Challenge and Related Matters," *Human Rights Quarterly*, 19(3), 461-509.

Rawls, J. (1971), *A Theory of Justice* (Cambridge, MA: Harvard University Press).

Rest, J.R. (1986), *Moral Development: Advances in Research and Theory* (New York: Praeger).

Robin, D.P. and R.E. Reidenbach (1993), "Searching For a Place to Stand: Toward a Workable Ethical Philosophy for Marketing," *Journal of Public Policy and Marketing*, 12(1), 97-105.

Rogers, H.P., A.O. Ogbuehi and C.M. Kochunny (1995), "Ethics and Transnational Corporations in Developing Countries: A Social Contract Perspective," *Journal of Euromarketing*, 4(2), 11-38.

Sen, A. (1997), "Human Rights and Asian Values," *The New Republic*, July 14 and 21, 33-40.

Shepard, J.M., M.G. Goldsby and V.W. Gerde (1997), "Teaching Business Ethics Through Literature," *Teaching Business Ethics*, 1(1), 33-51.

Steidlmeier, P. (1997), "Business Ethics and Politics in China," *Business Ethics*, 7(3), 131-143.

Steinmann, H. and A.G. Scherer (1997), "Intercultural Management Between Universalism and Relativism-Fundamental Problems in International Business Ethics and the Contribution of Recent German Philosophical Approaches," in S. Urban (ed.) *Europe in the Global Competition: Problems-Markets-Strategies* (Wiesbaden, Germany: Gabler), pp. 77-143.

Takahashi, A. (1997), "Ethics in Developing Economies of Asia," *Business Ethics Quarterly*, 7(3), 33-45.

Toyne, B. and D. Nigh (1997), *International Business: An Emerging Vision* (Columbia, SC: University of South Carolina Press).

Toyne, B. and D. Nigh (1998), "A More Expansive View of International Business," *Journal of International Business Studies*, 29(4), 863-876.

United Nations (1948), *Universal Declaration of Human Rights*. New York: United Nations.

Van Luijk, H.J.L. (1990), "Recent Developments in European Business Ethics," *Journal of Business Ethics*, 9(7), 537-544.

Velasquez, M. (1995), "International Business Ethics: The Aluminum Companies in Jamaica," *Business Ethics Quarterly*, 5(4), 865-882.

Vogel, D. (1993), "Is U.S. Business Obsessed with Ethics?" *Across the Board*, 30 (November-December), 31-33.

Getting Around the Impasse:
A Grounded Approach to Teaching Ethics and Social Responsibility in International Business Education

Marc T. Jones
Peter Lok

SUMMARY. The task of teaching ethics and social responsibility in international business courses is seemingly condemned to a positionality characterized by either an ethnocentric absolutism or a tolerant but unengaging relativism. This paper offers a strategy out of the absolutism-relativism impasse based on developing a grounded understanding of the elements, processes, and properties of capitalism. This common understanding can provide the base upon which informed dialogue, debate, and learning about topics associated with the ethical dimension of international business activity can be promoted. *[Article copies available for a fee from The Haworth Document Delivery Service: 1-800-342-9678. E-mail address: getinfo@haworthpressinc.com <Website: http://www. haworthpressinc.com>]*

KEYWORDS. Business ethics, social responsibility, international business education, capitalism, teaching ethics

---

Marc T. Jones is with the Department of Management and Employment Relations at the University of Auckland, Private Bag 92019, Auckland, New Zealand (E-mail: mt.jones@auckland.ac.nz). Peter Lok is with the Australian Graduate School of Management at University of Sydney and University of New South Wales, Sydney, NSW 2006, Australia.

[Haworth co-indexing entry note]: "Getting Around the Impasse: A Grounded Approach to Teaching Ethics and Social Responsibility in International Business Education." Jones, Marc T., and Peter Lok. Co-published simultaneously in *Journal of Teaching in International Business* (International Business Press, an imprint of The Haworth Press, Inc.) Vol. 11, No. 1, 1999, pp. 21-42; and *Teaching International Business: Ethics and Corporate Social Responsibility* (ed: Gopalkrishnan R. Iyer) International Business Press, an imprint of The Haworth Press, Inc., 1999, pp. 21-42. Single or multiple copies of this article are available for a fee from The Haworth Document Delivery Service [1-800-342-9678, 9:00 a.m. - 5:00 p.m. (EST). E-mail address: getting@haworthpressinc.com].

INTRODUCTION:
THE ABSOLUTISM-RELATIVISM IMPASSE

Teaching ethical material is always difficult, particularly in areas such as international business. This difficulty is compounded as student bodies become increasingly diverse in terms of their sociocultural composition. In such circumstances, the inherent problems of taking an absolutist ethical perspective are compounded by an obvious ethnocentrism. Meanwhile, the utility of a consequentialist approach is undermined by the difficulties of establishing any consensus regarding means and ends across various sociocultural divides. The result is usually–seemingly inevitably–a default to a position of neutered relativism regarding not only actions and their outcomes but, increasingly, even over the very *meanings* of actions and outcomes. While such an approach can promote a form of uncaring, uninterested toleration for difference, it does nothing to establish a common understanding from which issues, policies, and outcomes can be actively debated by engaged participants. Many teachers and students recognize the unsatisfactory and unsatisfying state of affairs this leaves us in, but what can be done about it short of privileging one group's understanding above all others?

The strategy taken here is to address the absolutism-relativism impasse by side-stepping it to some extent through developing a foundational understanding of the basic elements, processes, and properties of capitalism. This logic is based on an acceptance of the inevitable 'truth' of relativism with respect to concepts such as ethics and social responsibility. Such concepts have to be understood in their own terms according to their particular meanings within the sociocultural contexts within which they are embedded and have historically developed.

Yet, underlying socioculturally contingent notions of 'good' and 'bad' or 'right' and 'wrong' are the more solid material structures and processes associated with capitalism, particularly in cases where localities are tightly connected to global capitalism through trade, investment, and/or subcontracting linkages. These structures and processes unfold with certain regularities and effects which can be understood and agreed upon by people from otherwise incommensurable (or incomprehensible) sociocultural positionalities. It is these aspects of capitalism that are targeted in the pedagogical strategy elaborated in this paper.

Once a grounded understanding of capitalism is established, the various economic, political, sociocultural, technological, and environmental issues associated with international business activity can then be discussed from this common epistemological foundation. This common base allows otherwise diverse perspectives on issues such as the role of state vs. market to communicate and debate with each other, which promotes not only tolerance but *interest* and *learning*.

This paper proceeds in four main sections. In the first the key elements, processes, and properties associated with capitalist political economy are outlined. The second looks to Adam Smith to examine both the ethical justification and the systemic dysfunctions associated with classical capitalism. The third examines ethics and social responsibility in different sociocultural and business system contexts. The fourth examines various developments associated with globalization in order to generate some key ethical and social issues which are–or should be–of concern to all scholars and students of international business.

UNDERSTANDING CAPITALIST POLITICAL ECONOMY

Following Jones (1996a), capitalism is an economic system based upon private property, production for profit, wage labor, and the use of the market mechanism for allocating a society's productive resources efficiently. Capitalism is all about seeking profits by (a) avoiding or eliminating competition, (b) maximizing organizational productivity, and (c) socializing the costs of production. Generally profits are sought through some combination of (a)-(c), the specifics of which are contingent on factors such as market structure, the nature and cost of available technologies, and the degree of influence over the state available to capitalist interests. Importantly, as capital, product, and labor markets integrate across national borders (e.g., the European Union) these factors increasingly assume a transnational character.

In terms of its essential characteristics and institutional logic, the capitalist firm is not a complex entity; indeed its fundamental rationality has remained unchanged since the advent of capitalism some two centuries ago. Any capitalist firm essentially represents a package of human, physical and capital resources which have been organized for a single overriding purpose: the pursuit of profit (or capital accumulation) for its owners. In this endeavor, society provides critical resources (e.g., customers, legitimacy) which the firm must secure for survival and growth; employees are a key organizational resource to be utilized effectively; and customers' needs are to be met (as well as created) as a means to secure profits.

Unquestionably, contemporary capitalism is more complex than in previous decades due to the increase in size and operational scope of business organizations–e.g., the largest transnational corporations (TNCs) generate revenues in excess of many nation-states' gross domestic products (Korten, 1995)–as well as the growing complexity of stakeholder claims on these organizations (see Sutton, 1993). Furthermore, as Perrow (1986) observes, large bureaucratic firms pursue the logic of capital accumulation imperfectly due to problems of managerial control resulting from the combination of bounded rationality and conflicting intra-organizational interests. Although these complicating factors suggest that the pure logic of capital accumulation is unable to fully manifest itself in any real business firm, they do not in any way undermine our central point that any capitalist organization's fundamental raison d'etre remains the pursuit of profits.

The imperative to avoid or eliminate competition can at some times foster cutthroat competition, at other times substantial cooperation, even formal collusion. The particular dynamics of industry structure would seem to determine which of the above forms of competitive orientation is optimum for a given firm (Shughart, 1990). The historical development from competitive to monopoly capitalism has been richly described in the Marxist literature (Baran and Sweezy, 1966; DuBoff, 1989), as well as in more conventional accounts (Chandler, 1977). Certainly the atomistic, competitive markets envisioned by Adam Smith as being socially efficient (by prescribing market power and promoting consumer sovereignty) rarely exist today. For example, Dicken (1998) notes the extent to which global commodity markets are highly concentrated and dominated by a relative handful of powerful transnational corporations. Yet these TNCs relate to each other in complex webs of interdependence, cooperation, and collusion as well as competition (see Best, 1990).

The imperative to maximize organizational productivity fosters investment in new technologies of various types. Some of these relate to broad ways of organizing the production process and the wider organizational structure within which this process is embedded. Examples here would include the transformation from functional to multidivisional structures as firms diversified into new product-market areas (Chandler, 1977), as well as the contemporary emphasis by large firms on contracting-out peripheral activities to network-linked suppliers (see Harrison, 1994). Other technologies are more hardware-oriented and refer to the replacement of human labor with capital equipment through automation, along with the widespread adoption of flexible manufacturing systems which enable firms to exploit economies of scope by producing a range of related products to serve fragmented markets (Piore and Sabel, 1984). Still other types of technologies are concerned with enhancing management control over the labor process within firms. Zuboff's (1989) work richly illustrates both the emancipatory and coercive potential of the new information and communications technologies which have entered the workplace over the last generation.

An effective pedagogical strategy to address some of the social and ethical issues raised by the various forms of organizational restructuring is to present restructuring efforts as broadly constituting either 'high road' or 'low road' approaches to achieving competitiveness in increasingly dynamic and internationalized markets. 'Low road' approaches focus on reducing costs primarily through labor intensification–getting people to work harder for the same or fewer rewards. Intensification is achieved by slashing wages, downgrading benefits and working conditions, and multi-tasking (eliminating any labor downtime; giving people more responsibility to perform a variety of mundane tasks). We refer to this approach as the 'low road' as it is a largely negative approach which is based on attaining competitiveness through a *wealth transfer* from wages to profits, rather than through any significant investment in firm infrastructure or upgrading of organizational resources designed to increase the value-added. Conversely, 'high road' strategies involve investing in organizational resources of all kinds (human and technical) to maximize the value of those resources, which can then transfer their increased value to throughput in terms of more efficient production and better performing products. These approaches often focus on employees as the key to promoting sustainable competitiveness through *wealth creation*. Here we find genuine multi-skilling (giving workers multiple and complementary skills), serious and respectful communication between workers and managers, and the promotion of an organizational atmosphere of symbiosis and reciprocity.

The imperative to improve their cost structures versus domestic and foreign competitors means that firms will have strong incentives to minimize or avoid as many costs involved with production as possible. Negative effects of the industrial process are thus externalized (or socialized) onto society rather than contained by the firms producing them and incorporated into the price of finished products. At a societal level this means that more goods and services are produced and consumed than is socially efficient. This is because goods and services are underpriced–they do not reflect the full costs incurred in their production–and are thus consumed at an excessive rate (assuming some degree of positive demand elasticity). Significantly, the negative externalities created by business firms socializing the costs of production are not limited to environmental degradation; firms also do not bear the human costs of production. By that we mean that firms are not held responsible for the negative effects on those of their employees who labor under alienating conditions, whether these be the result of deskilling, intensification, insecurity or other related phenomena (cf. Hamper, 1991). Clearly, were products priced by capitalist firms to include their 'true' costs of production, the overall economic efficiency of a capitalist system would be highly questionable. And this is exactly what we turn to question in the classroom, usually in a series of formal or informal debates with students taking sides on the merits of capitalism vs. both some idealized 'other' system as well as vs. currently or previously existing systems (e.g., Cuban socialism, tribal bartering systems).

Having established a foundational (if debatable) understanding of capitalist political economy, the next section draws on Adam Smith's insights in order to raise some ethical issues associated with the origins of capitalism as well as with the actual or potential dysfunctions of the system in action. The point of using Smith here, rather than Marx, is that it allows students a less threatening entry point into critique and debate from the insights of capitalism's greatest historical advocate, rather than from its greatest opponent.

ADAM SMITH AND CAPITALISM

Capitalism has been interpreted as constituting a moral, immoral, or amoral system by social and economic theorists of various ideological persuasions. For example, proponents of capitalism stress the aspects of consumer sovereignty, individual choice and responsibility, material progress, allocative efficiency, and (in some cases) even theological virtuousness (see Novak, 1982). Critics of capitalism, on the other hand, focus on such negative aspects as the exploitation of labor, hyper-materialism, waste and environmental degradation, and a chronically unequal distribution of resources (Bowles and Gintis, 1986). Other observers maintain that capitalism is simply one of a variety of ways of organizing a nation's economic affairs and that it should be judged simply on its ability to allocate resources in such a way as to sustain and extend a comparatively high standard-of-living for the average citizen (Heilbroner, 1985).

Each of the preceding perspectives has its merits as well as its drawbacks, yet each also largely ignores the normative orientation of Adam Smith as he developed the framework for a capitalist economic system over two centuries ago. The period in which Smith completed *The Wealth of Nations* (Smith, 1980), was known as the Mercantilist Era. Mercantilism was an economic system geared to maximize the power of the nation-state (itself a relatively new institutional form) relative to other nation-states through pursuit of autarky (i.e., self-sufficiency). The mercantilist state attempted to maximize its exports while minimizing its imports from other states with which it was competing. Colonial possessions supplied the mercantilist state with raw materials as well as markets for its finished goods. In its quest for autarky, mercantilist political economy required a high degree of administrative centralization; it was thus consistent with nondemocratic political institutions as well as noncompetitive (i.e., monopolistic) domestic economic structures. Mercantilism benefited producers and entrenched interests at the expense of consumers and the growing middle classes, who were forced to pay inflated prices for domestically produced goods which were shielded from foreign competition by various protectionist mechanisms.

Smith developed his model of a market driven, consumer-based economic system as an alternative to the political economy of mercantilism. Whereas mercantilism involved consumers subsidizing producers in a system of centralized (and thus authoritarian) economic and political structures, Smith envisioned a production system organized according to the consumer's interests (expressed as demand). Further, this new decentralized economic system oriented to maximizing the welfare of the economic consumer by providing goods and services according to the market forces of supply and demand would be compatible with a democratic political system oriented to maximizing the welfare of the citizen as a political consumer.

The political economy Smith was advocating was thus based on maximizing consumer/citizen choice in both economic and political spheres. Smith's paradigm shifted the institutional emphasis from centralized to decentralized structures, from authoritarianism to representative democracy, from monopoly to competitive markets, from autarky to international interdependence through a spatially expanding division of labor, and from producer appropriation of the societal surplus to consumer sovereignty. His system, which would later be called "capitalism," was as revolutionary a concept with respect to the dominant mercantilism of its day as Marx's communism was to the capitalism of the mid-nineteenth century.

Yet Smith also envisioned several potential weaknesses of his model. Jones (1993) discusses five moral problems Smith associated with capitalism: impoverishing the spirit of the workers and the work ethic more generally, creating cities in which anonymity facilitated price-fixing, expanding the ranks of the idle rich, inducing government to foster monopolies and selective privileges, and separating ownership and control as the scale and capital requirements of business firms increased. We now turn to discuss some of Smith's most significant fears about the potential dysfunctions of the system he conceptualized and normatively advocated.

Perhaps the dysfunction Smith feared most was the concentration of economic resources by monopolistic joint-stock corporations. He wrote at length about the abuses of such monopolistic joint-stock companies as the East India Company, the Hudson's Bay Company, and the South Sea Company. As noted by Ginzberg (1979:41), "Smith's concerns about the evils of monopoly went beyond the unjustified rewards that accrued to the man who was able to rig the market. A still more untoward consequence of monopoly was the ineffective management that in Smith's view was the likely concomitant of an entrepreneur's being sheltered from the cold winds of competition."

Smith also expected that concentrated economic resources could be readily translated into political influence, which he considered similar to other commodities for which there was a supply and demand. He was particularly scathing with regard to the political powers exercised by powerful economic interests. He warned that legislative proposals emanating from the business sector

> Ought always to be listened to with great precaution, and ought never be adopted till after having been long and carefully examined, not only with the most scrupulous, but with the most suspicious attention. [Such legislation] comes from an order of men, whose interest is never exactly the same with that of the public, who have generally an interest to deceive and even to oppress the public, and who accordingly have, upon many occasions, both deceived and oppressed it. (1980: 359)

Smith's advocacy of an economic system based on small producers, each lacking the ability to affect prices through the exercise of market power, thus had direct political implications. Competitive markets would ensure that no producer assumed a dominant position from which it could influence the market either directly (through price-fixing, predatory pricing, etc.) or indirectly (through privileges obtained from political influence).

Interestingly, non-American students seem to more readily take Smith's observations to heart than do Americans socialized with assumptions of institutional pluralism and the rigid separation of the economic from the political in their 'democratic-capitalist' society. For example, when following Lindbloom (1977) or Reich (1998) in raising the question of the appropriateness and desirability of extending corporate 'personhood' into the political realm, Hong Kong Chinese or Indonesian students are more likely to recognize the actual or potential problems associated with this legalized fiction than are most Americans. Interesting debates can also be generated on the issue of the desirability vs. the reality of institutional pluralism and the separation of politics from economics.

Smith also recognized the necessity of a strong work ethic to provide the twin dynamics for increasing productivity and accelerating capital accumulation. In this vein, he noted that, "Capitals are increased by parsimony [frugality], and diminished by prodigality and misconduct" (1980: 437). As the worker became more productive, better paid, and saw his standard-of-living rise, however, he demanded more leisure time and engaged in increasingly conspicuous consumption. This shift in emphasis from the virtues of productivity, frugality, and responsibility to leisure and consumption-related activities undermined the basic normative and behavioral foundations of classical capitalism (see also Bell, 1973). This point can be fruitfully addressed when the class composition is multinational, particularly if there is significant Asian representation–i.e., as Asia industrializes, are younger generations becoming 'Americanized' in terms of their work, leisure, and consumption habits in a way which undermines the very basis of the region's heretofore successful industrialization?

Smith also recognized the inevitability of market failure in the provisioning of public goods and the consequent need for government intervention to ensure that services that could not be rendered profitably (e.g., fire protection) because of free-rider problems would nonetheless be available to the public. As Rosenberg (1979:27) observes, "there is nothing in Smith that is inherently opposed to legislation of a protective nature or to restrictions upon the natural liberty of individuals, where such restrictions are likely to advance important social goals." Of course, the alternative to universal, publicly funded provisioning of essential services is selective, privatized provisioning of those services on an ability-to-pay basis. This exclusionary method of supplying what Smith would have defined normatively as universally essential services was (and is) contrary to the progressive nature of his paradigm. This issue effectively lends itself to class debate, particularly when continental Europeans and Asian students from the so-called 'development states' are joined with Anglo-Saxon students from New Right-oriented states and societies.

Finally, Smith perceived the threat the ever-increasing capitalist division of labor posed to the humanity of the working classes. The routinization of work and the progressive deskilling of the worker made possible by segmentation and specialization processes threatened to create a society of automatons with few skills, interests, or objectives save the vulgar pursuit of the pleasure principle. Smith feared that the division of labor would drive most men to be

> As stupid and ignorant as it is possible for a human creature to become. The torpor of his [the worker's] mind renders him, not only incapable of relishing or bearing a part in any rational conversation, but in conceiving any generous, noble or tender sentiment, and consequently of forming any just judgement concerning many even of the ordinary duties of private life . . . [specialization] seems in this sense to be acquired at the expense

of his intellectual, social, and martial virtues. But in every improved and civilized society this is the state into which the laboring poor, that is, the great body of the people, must necessarily fall, *unless government takes some pains to prevent this.* (1980: 50; italics added)

To attenuate the dehumanization attendant with the capitalist division of labor, Smith advocated government investment in public education. Importantly, and consistent with Smith's larger moral project, an educated population was also a fundamental prerequisite for the functioning of a democratic political system. This particular topic is a fascinating one to broach in classes with multinational students, particularly those with Asian backgrounds which have come from cultures which have valued and emphasized education but not civil liberties, democratic freedoms, or representative political systems. These students' perspectives can be compared and contrasted with those of Western (and especially Anglo-Saxon) students who have grown up in societies which stress democracy and civil rights but tend to (comparatively and increasingly) underinvest in public goods such as education and social welfare.

Having reviewed some of the classical justifications for and dysfunctions associated with capitalism as identified by Adam Smith, in the next section we turn to examine the topic of ethics and social responsibility in different cultural contexts. That is, how do 'capital logic,' ethics, and social responsibility manifest when they are embedded in different business systems? And can we expect these differences to lessen in the future as globalization progresses and institutional structures and business systems converge to a narrower range of configurations?

ETHICS AND SOCIAL RESPONSIBILITY IN DIFFERENT CONTEXTS

The core of the concept of social responsibility is somewhat elusive. At a general level we can accept Wood's (1991: 695) thinking that "the basic idea of corporate social responsibility is that business and society are interwoven rather than distinct entities; therefore, society has certain expectations for appropriate business behavior and outcomes." Wood proceeds to discuss social responsibility in terms of its structural principles and outcomes. She identifies three structural principles: legitimacy, public responsibility and managerial discretion. Legitimacy is operative at the institutional level and refers to the nature of the relationship between business and society and specifies what is expected of any individual business because of its institutional membership. Public responsibility focuses on the outcomes of a business's activity as constituting another scope of that business's responsibility. The exact specification of public responsibility will thus vary with each firm and its specific relationship with its environment. Managerial discretion is oriented to individual managers and decision makers and emphasizes their responsibility to behave as moral actors and promote (within the structural constraints in which they operate) socially responsible outcomes.

Central to this paper's concerns is the fact that the three principles and outcomes Wood identifies will inevitably carry different meanings across different contexts. The particular manner in which social responsibility is constructed as a concept and then practiced in real organizations can be expected to vary according to issues operative at several levels, including the nature of the sociocultural formation, the configuration of the national business system, as well as industry and firm-level considerations (see Jones, 1998). In this discussion we will focus on the first two levels.

At the sociocultural level the primary issue is the manner in which the capitalist discourse is inflected in the social structure and normative system. Some inflections of capitalism might be more supportive of social responsibility, others less so. Capitalism is, after all, a socially constructed system of signs, meanings and actions, although once set in motion it does behave in predictable ways and becomes reified in a given institutional structure (Deetz, 1992). The way in which capitalism (in terms of its associated institutional structures and social relations) is introduced to a country, and the nature of the pre-existing order onto which it is grafted, are of major significance in determining the particular capitalistic inflection of a sociocultural system (Cardoso and Faletto, 1979). For example, settler colonies such as Australia and New Zealand have had qualitatively different developmental experiences than the numerous imperial colonies in Asia, Africa, and Latin America, resulting in widely different social constructions of what the legitimate role of business in society is and should be.

Until recently, capitalism was understood to be inherently individualistic in terms of its institutional incentives and cultural correlates. This was largely derived from the exclusivist nature of private property and the individuated acts of work and consumption (Bowles and Gintis, 1985). However, in recent works examining Asian capitalism, Whitley (1992) and Fukuyama (1995) (albeit in very different ways) assert that this conceptualization of capitalism as an ontologically individualistic system is incorrect and is itself an historically contingent, culturally inflected construction characteristic of the manner in which capitalism has evolved in the West. They note that Asian capitalism exhibits substantially different notions of individual identity as well as different institutions promoting trust and reciprocity. These themes are pursued at lower levels of analysis by Chu (1995) and Hofstede (1984). Chu examines the Asian business mind-set as a whole in contrast to Western approaches to transacting business, as well as differences between the Chinese, Japanese, and Korean business cultures. Hofstede's work is based on his seminal investigations of national culture differences along four dimensions: power-distance, uncertainty avoidance, individualism, and masculinity. Of particular relevance here is his finding that the Asian countries in his sample all scored very low on the individualism dimension, while the United States rated as the *most* individualistic nation.

The manner in which the capitalist discourse articulates with other major societal discourses is also significant. For example, Bowles and Gintis (1985) have addressed the relationship between capitalism and democracy in the United States in terms of a clash between the discourses of property rights (capitalism) and citizenship rights (democracy). The discourse of property rights centers on the notion of ownership, which is essentially the right to exclude secondary stakeholders from participation in proprietary processes or outcomes. The discourse of citizenship, conversely, is at its core inclusive in nature; it seeks to extend participation to all members of society in those matters that effect them.

Bowles and Gintis note that traditionally in American society the property rights discourse has dominated economic affairs while the citizenship discourse has been based in the political sphere. They argue that this allocation of discourses to separate institutional spheres has constituted a contingent–not inevitable–historical development with tremendous distributional implications. The intensely political nature of the hierarchical relations of the workplace are generally conceptualized through the property rights discourse. Thus, the fact that management constitutes the legal representative of ownership interests enables it to decide what's what in the firm; secondary stakeholders such as employees and communities have only tenuous legal status in terms of challenging managerial prerogatives.

In other nations the nature of the articulation between the discourses of capitalism and democracy are considerably different. For example, in South Korea the capitalist discourse predated the democratic one, which only began to emerge in the 1980s. Meanwhile, in Russia the two discourses were introduced almost simultaneously on a population which had little understanding of the content or institutional implications of either. The point is that students from diverse sociocultural backgrounds will have qualitatively different experiences, understandings, and normative orientations to issues such as the optimum relationship between economy and society, or the desirability (or feasibility) of democracy. These differences can provide rich discussions as students are encouraged to relate their own experiences and opinions to their classmates. While definitive answers or resolutions of core debates will be elusive, the very act of addressing such topics in class constitutes an enriching educational experience.

Turning to the national level, the key influences on social responsibility here include the level of modernization or economic development of a nation and the particular institutional arrangements it exhibits. There is considerable evidence to suggest that the more developed a society is the more prominent the social responsibility discourse will be (Cannon, 1994). This is illustrated by the existence and enforcement of national regulatory standards in the areas of environmental protection and/or workplace safety, which systematically vary according to the level of national economic development (see Kennedy, 1993; Vogel, 1995). This effect seems to be true across the board with respect to the ability of secondary stakeholders (e.g., employees, communities) to assert claims on business activity. It is also intuitively comprehensible: a society first needs to satisfy its members' basic needs for adequate food, shelter and the like before it can address higher level needs in areas such as aesthetics, actualization at work, or long-term environmental sustainability. But is this in fact correct? A contra point could be made that the more developed a society is, the more there is a need for a social responsibility discourse–i.e., that economic development increases social *irresponsibility*, thus fostering a need to address social responsibility issues (Iyer, 1998). Addressing these questions in the classroom makes for a wide-ranging and stimulating discussion, one which is accessible from many perspectives and student backgrounds.

Rawls (1993) uses the term 'basic structure' to refer to a given country's institutional arrangements in politics, law, economics, and the family. These arrangements provide the background conditions against which the actions of individuals and associations take place. Clearly, variations of these arrangements can have a profound effect on the contours of a nation's business culture and the manner in which the social roles of owner, manager, employee, consumer, and citizen are constituted. Hofstede's (1996) recent work further establishes the fundamental linkages between institutional order and sociocultural orientation. Particular national institutional arrangements can either actively promote social responsibility, latently sustain it, or actively discourage it.

Perhaps more useful than Rawls' rather abstract 'basic structure' is Whitley's (1992) notion of the 'business system.' The business system represents a given national institutional context and is likely to affect substantively, at the level of the individual firm located in such a system, both its relative competitiveness and the manner in which it competes, as well as notions of business ethics and social responsibility. The business system of a country includes the financial system, industry structure, industry collectives, industrial relations system, political system, legal and regulatory system, military, and knowledge superstructures. Several distinct types of business systems are distinguishable. For example, Orru (1997) identifies alliance, digriste (state dominated), and familial-type business systems, while some observers in the popular press refer to 'casino capitalism' on Wall Street, 'gangster capitalism' in Russia, and 'crony capitalism' in Asia as terms indicative of particular types of business systems.

Although business systems interact, principally through trade and investment activities, each is to a significant degree unique in its overall configuration (see Hollingsworth and Boyer, 1997). However, Whitley (1992:254) provides an account of particular factors which can promote convergence between business systems. Over the past few decades there have appeared many important signs of convergence between business systems (Jones and Venkatesh, 1996), at least within particular types of such systems. Importantly, this convergence generally takes the form of a subordinate system becoming isomorphic with a dominant (or hegemonic) one.

In classroom situations it has proven useful to query students as to their opinions on the business system/institutional convergence issue–i.e., to what extent could or should we expect business practices, organizational systems and structures, and management approaches to become more similar across different countries and cultures? And would the dominant model(s) be American, Western, and/or some synthesis of currently hegemonic institutional templates with Chinese, Indian, and/or other forms of political, social, and economic organization?

The previous sections have discussed the fundamentals of capitalist political economy, identified its potential dysfunctions, and addressed the importance of the particular way in which 'capital logic' inflects through specific and unique sociocultural formations and national business systems. The groundwork has thus been established from which numerous significant issues can be examined in terms of their ethical dimensions. The next section focuses on some key issues associated with globalization.

GLOBALIZATION AND ITS IMPACTS

Once a foundational understanding of capitalism and its contingent inflections through different sociocultural formations and business systems has been established, the ethical dimension of numerous issues relevant to international business can then be addressed. As globalization is a topic at the core of many international business courses, this section will identify and briefly elaborate some key social and ethical issues associated with the globalization process.

The globalization process appears to be promoting a dualistic form of capitalist economic development in the advanced countries. One component of this formation is a 'techno-economy' characterized by high-technology, automation, flexible systems, skilled labor, and the like (similar to the high-tech aspects of post-Fordism). The second component is a 'grunge economy' made up of generally downgraded labor (Sassen-Koob, 1984), which is itself bifurcated; firstly into a segment composed of semi-skilled workers employed on a contingent basis, largely in small firms acting as subcontractors to much larger corporates in the techno-economy (this contingent segment amounted to 25% of the American labor force in 1992 and is projected to increase to 35% in the year 2000 [Castells, 1996]); secondly into an underclass of unskilled and/or redundant labor working sporadically under extreme conditions in the informal sector (outside of the formally regulated and taxed economy). The contingent and informal elements of the grunge economy are characterized by the multiplicity of labor processes in evidence, including the revival of domestic, familial, and paternalistic labor systems totally unexpected in so-called 'advanced industrial economies.' Significantly, it is the new production, information, and communications technologies and forms of organization in the techno-economy which have permitted or driven these developments in the grunge economy.

The dynamic expansion of the techno-economy leaves more and more people out of its value and employment generating processes, widening the gap between haves and have-nots and increasing social fragmentation. This is because the techno-economy is far more efficient than its Fordist-Keynesian predecessor in containing positive externalities and directing its benefits to vested stakeholder groups–primarily owners, the professional-managerial classes, technically-skilled labor, and moneyed consumers. Other groups, most particularly the semi-skilled industrial working class which was effectively integrated into the mass production/ mass consumption calculus of Fordism-Keynesianism, are excluded from this particular form of economic growth.

It follows, then, that the expansion of the grunge economy is a *necessary* corollary to the continued growth of the techno-economy. Necessary firstly for those groups who are somehow excluded from the circuit of high value creation in the techno-economy and need primary or supplemental means to obtain the resources necessary for social reproduction in the contingent and/or informal segments of the grunge economy. Necessary also in order to prevent total social fragmentation and the ensuing violence which would disrupt wealth generation in the core techno-economy by securing at least a minimal amount of legitimation to the social order and the role of the state (see Standing, 1989).

The type of globalization process outlined above raises numerous significant social and ethical issues, relevant to advanced as well as developing and underdeveloped nations. Perhaps the most important stems from its exclusionary tendencies and concerns its implications for societal development. The key question here is whether a (formal or de facto) alliance of the capitalist, profession-al-managerial, and technically-skilled working classes will pursue a strategy of spatial and institutional containment of the underclass and/or one of self-containment within fortified communities, work-places, etc. Aspects of these developments are already clearly vis-ible in cities such as Los Angeles, where members of the techno-economy live within gated communities patrolled by private armed security, while the most downgraded members of the grunge econo-my are subjected to social and spatial 'dividing practices' (Fou-cault, 1979) through which they are contained in ethnic ghettoes defined by the configuration of housing prices, transportation corri-dors, infrastructural provision (or the lack thereof), and police sur-veillance patterns. The spaces between these groups are occupied by members of the contingent segment of the grunge economy (see Davis, 1990).

A linked question concerns what the reactions will be to increasing exclusion and disenfranchisement among those groups so effected? Important considerations here include the extent of systemic con-sciousness and understanding of these developments, the nature of class, racial, gender and other forms of identity and solidarity, and the existence of alternative narratives around which to organize for effec-tive political action. Given the current state of affairs in most advanced nations, the prospects for the formation of an effective political bloc of 'New Social Movements' would seem remote. An individuation of the effects of increasing social exclusion–and of the reactions to it in the form of violent and criminal activity (see Castells, 1998)–would seem more likely, along with a continuation and intensification of (necessar-ily fragmenting) interest-based politics. Overall, we might expect the 'Brazilianization' (Barnett and Muller, 1974) of advanced societies as massive and increasing social disparities and other attributes of chron-ically segmented social formations become normalized aspects of the cognitive and material landscapes.

Another related set of questions concerns the role of the state as the globalization process unfolds. As noted earlier, states have certainly lost some of their powers of economic management to both supra- and sub-national bodies. Yet they retain an essential monopoly over mili-tary force and the means of direct control over persons within their territories. Further, most (all?) advanced states have in recent years substantially increased the information they collect on individuals (*stat[e]*istics), expanded police powers, and rescinded various civil liberties and protections afforded to citizens and employees (see Jessop, 1994; Jones, 1996b). In fact, 'the state' seems to be evolving in a post-democratic direction, or possibly *de*volving to a pre-capitalist apparatus (as described by Foucault, 1979). Perhaps we are in the midst of transformation in which the state is becoming the primary institutional enforcement mechanism for global capital, while its other functions are either shifted to alternative institutions or terminated altogether?

Turning to the likely impact of globalization on major stakeholder groups, it should come as no surprise that some groups will benefit considerably while others will be substantially disadvantaged. Finance capital is the big winner, although it will also have to accommodate itself to chronic instability. Large industrial capital in the form of TNCs also benefits greatly, as do members of the professional-managerial class, technically-skilled workers, and moneyed consumers. Meanwhile, small-scale capital will either lose out or find itself at the whim of big capital, semi-skilled and unskilled workers will find themselves relegated to struggling in the contingent or informal segments of the grunge economy, and states will lose sovereignty to both multilateral and regional/local institutions.

Other ethical issues raised by globalization include deindustrialization; hyperconsumerism and environmental destruction; the continuing erosion of substantive democracy and the changing nature of citizenship from a universal political right to a matter of economic status and privilege; cultural imperialism and global-local tensions; and the implications of the numerous technological developments which transform our societies, organizations, and personal lives. How each of these issues can or does manifest in different sociocultural environments and business systems is a topic of much relevance and interest to most international business students, particularly in cases where class compositions are diverse.

Experience has shown that an effective way to broach these subjects to students is to first discuss the globalization process in terms of its related economic, political, and social effects as outlined above. Careful attention must be paid to country differences, as globalization has not impacted the United States in the same way as it has a small trading nation such as New Zealand. The lecturer can also draw upon the opinions and experiences of students from various nations as to how globalization has effected their home countries and whether or not they agree with the version of globalization depicted above. From there the discussion can proceed to deal with the social and ethical issues raised by globalization, such as whether students feel the benefits of globalization outweigh the costs, or if the particular distribution of costs and benefits is itself an issue that merits consideration. In our experience–and very much consistent with Hofstede's (1984) work– students typically differ quite substantially on such matters: continental Europeans (and particularly Scandinavians) are the most socially-minded; Americans (and Anglo-Saxons more generally) the most oriented to market outcomes and individual responsibility; and Asians (particularly overseas Chinese) very commercially-oriented and accepting of the negative externalities associated with market outcomes, but also displaying a strong sense of dedication to the well being of one's social network and (especially) family, as well as a desirability for overall social harmony.

CONCLUSION: A WAY OUT OF THE IMPASSE?

The task of teaching ethics and social responsibility in international business is seemingly condemned to a positionality characterized by either an ethnocentric absolutism or a tolerant but unengaging relativism. This paper offers a strategy out of this impasse based on developing a grounded understanding of the elements, processes, and properties of capitalism. This common understanding can provide the base upon which informed dialogue, debate, and learning about topics associated with the international business environment can be developed.

Rather than pursue a Kantian project of trying to derive ideal and universal ethical systems from the top-down, international business scholars would be better advised to work from the ground-up. This involves examining–from an understanding of capitalism and 'capital logic'–how different ethical systems arise within their unique sociocultural contexts; how these articulate within their relevant national business systems; and how these systems interact across the shrinking space-time matrix of contemporary capitalism in its globalizing phase.

The approach elaborated in this paper has developed over ten years of teaching business ethics and social responsibility to socioculturally diverse students in the United States, New Zealand, Australia, and Hong Kong. Of course not all those who teach ethics and/or social responsibility in international business courses will find it useful. What is inarguable, though, is that the more diverse the sociocultural background of the student body, the more important it is to try to find *some* solid conceptual base upon which to promote not only tolerance but also interest, engagement, and learning.

REFERENCES

Baran, P. and P. Sweezy. 1966. *Monopoly Capital* (Monthly Review Press, NY).

Barnett, R. and R. Muller. 1974. *Global Reach* (Simon & Schuster, NY).

Bell, D. 1973. *The Cultural Contradictions of Capitalism.* (Basic Books, NY).

Best, M. 1990. *The New Competition* (Free Press, NY).

Bowles, S. and H. Gintis. 1985. *Democracy and Capitalism* (Basic Books, NY).

Cannon, T. 1994. *Corporate Responsibility* (Pitman Publishing, London).

Cardoso, F. and E. Faletto. 1979. *Dependency and Development in Latin America* (University of California Press, Berkeley).

Castells, M. 1996. *The Rise of the Network Society* (Blackwell, Oxford).

Castells, M. 1998. *End of Millenium* (Blackwell, Oxford).

Chandler, A.D. 1977. *The Visible Hand* (Free Press, NY).

Chu, C. 1995. *The Asian Mind Game* (Stealth Productions, Australia).

Davis, M. 1990. *City of Quartz* (Verso, London).

Deetz, S. 1992. *Democracy in an Age of Corporate Colonization* (SUNY Press, Albany, NY).

Dicken, P. 1998. *Global Shift* (Paul Chapman, London).

DuBoff, R.B. 1989. *Accumulation and Power* (M.E. Sharpe, Inc., Armonk, NY).

Foucault, M. 1979. *Discipline and Punish* (Pantheon, NY).

Fukuyama, F. 1995. *Trust* (H. Hamilton, London).

Ginzberg, E. 1979. 'An Economy Formed by Men.' In G. O'Driscoll (Ed.), *Adam Smith and Modern Political Economy* (Iowa State University Press, Ames, Iowa).

Hamper, B. 1991. *Rivethead* (Warner Books, NY).

Harrison, B. 1994. *Lean and Mean* (Basic Books, NY).

Heilbroner, R. 1985. *The Nature and Logic of Capitalism* (Basic Books, NY).

Hofstede, G. 1984. *Culture's Consequences: International Differences in Work-Related Attitudes* (Beverley Hills, Sage).

Hofstede, G. 1996. 'An American in Paris: The Influence of Nationality on Organization Theories.' *Organization Studies*, 17(3), 525-537.

Hollingsworth, J. and R. Boyer. 1997. *Contemporary Capitalism* (University of Chicago Press, Chicago).

Iyer, G. 1998. Personal correspondence.

Jessop, B. 1994. 'Post-Fordism and the State.' In Amin, A. (ed.), *Post-Fordism* (Blackwell, London) pp. 251-279.

Jones, M. 1993. 'Adam Smith and the Ethics of Contemporary Democratic Capitalism in New Zealand.' *International Journal of Social Economics*, 20 (12), 3-12.

Jones, M. 1996a. 'Missing the Forest for the Trees: A Critique of the Social Responsibility Concept and Discourse.' *Business and Society*, 35 (1).

Jones, M. 1996b. 'Institutions of Global Restructuring.' Unpublished manuscript.

Jones, M. 1998. 'The Institutional Determinants of Social Responsibility.' *Journal of Business Ethics*, forthcoming.

Jones, M. and A. Venkatesh. 1996. 'A Critical Analysis of the Role of the Multinational Corporation in Global Marketing and Consumption.' In R. Belk, N. Dholakia, and A. Venkatesh (Eds.), *Consumption and Marketing: Macro Dimensions* (South-Western College Publishers, Cincinnatti).

Kennedy, P. 1993. *Preparing for the Twenty First Century* (Random House, NY).

Korten, D. 1995. *When Corporations Rule the World* (Kumarian Press, West Hartford, CN).

Lindblom, C.E. 1977. *Politics and Markets* (Basic Books, NY).

Novak, M. 1982. *The Spirit of Democratic Capitalism* (Free Press, NY).

Orru, M. 1997. 'The Institutional Analysis of Capitalist Economies.' In M. Orru, N. Biggart, and G. Hamilton, *The Economic Organization of East Asian Capitalism* (Sage, London).

Perrow, C. 1986. *Complex Organizations: A Critical Essay* (Random House, NY).

Piore, M. and C. Sabel. 1984. *The Second Industrial Divide* (Basic Books, NY).

Rawls, J. 1993. *Political Liberalism* (Columbia University Press, NY).

Reich, R. 1998. 'Private Corporations and Public Policy.' *California Management Review* 23(2), 56-68.

Rosenberg, N. 1979. 'Adam Smith and Laissez-faire Revisited.' In G. O'Driscoll (Ed.), *Adam Smith and Modern Political Economy* (Iowa State University Press, Ames, Iowa).

Sassen-Koob, S. 1984. 'Growth and Informalization at the Core.' In *The Urban Informal Sector* (Department of Sociology, Johns Hopkins University) pp. 492-518.

Shughart, W. 1990. *The Organization of Industry* (Irwin Press, Homewood, Illinois.).

Smith, A. 1980. *The Wealth of Nations* (Penguin, London).

Standing, G. 1989. 'The British Experiment.' In M. Portes, M. Castells, and L. Benton, *The Informal Economy* (Johns Hopkins University Press, Baltimore) pp. 279-297.

Sutton, B. 1993. 'Comment on Robert Monks: Is Institutional Investor Hegemony a Viable Legitimating Alternative?' In B. Sutton (Ed.), *The Legitimate Corporation* (Blackwell, Oxford).

Vogel, D. 1995. *Trading Up: Consumer and Environmental Regulation in a Global Economy* (Harvard University Press, Cambridge).

Whitley, R. 1992. *Business Systems in East Asia* (Sage, London).

Wood, D.J. 1991. 'Corporate Social Performance Revisited.' *Academy of Management Review* 16(4), 691-718.

Zuboff, S. 1989. *In the Age of the Smart Machine* (Free Press, NY).

Ethics in International Business Education: Perspectives from Five Business Disciplines

Debbie Thorne LeClair
Robert Clark
Linda Ferrell
Gilbert "Joe" Joseph
Daniel LeClair

SUMMARY. Ethics in international business is highly complex and requires an understanding of both business practice and cultural expectations. For this reason, business educators are seeking information on ethical issues, practices, and appropriate teaching content for the international business curriculum. In this paper, we examine international ethics issues and perspectives from the vantage point of five disciplines in business education, including economics, management, finance, accounting and marketing. Business educators can use this collection of

---

Debbie Thorne LeClair is Assistant Professor of Marketing and Director, Center for Ethics for the College of Business (E-mail: dthorne@alpha.utampa.edu), Robert Clark is Associate Professor of Finance and Director, Graduate Studies in Business at the College of Business (E-mail: rclark@alpha.utampa.edu), Gilbert "Joe" Joseph is Associate Professor of Accounting, College of Business (E-mail: gjoseph@alpha.utampa.edu), and Daniel LeClair is Associate Professor of Economics of the College of Business (E-mail: dleclair@alpha.utampa.edu), The University of Tampa. Linda Ferrell is with the Department of Marketing at College of Business Administration, University of Northern Colorado, Greeley, CO 80639 (E-mail: ocferrell@aol.com).
Please address correspondence to Debbie Thorne LeClair, The University of Tampa, 401 W. Kennedy Boulevard, Box 617, Tampa, FL 33606-1490 .
The authors thank the special volume editor and two anonymous reviewers for their helpful comments and suggestions.

[Haworth co-indexing entry note]: "Ethics in International Business Education: Perspectives from Five Business Disciplines." Leclair, Debbie Thorne et al. Co-published simultaneously in *Journal of Teaching in International Business* (International Business Press, an imprint of The Haworth Press, Inc.) Vol. 11, No. 1, 1999, pp. 43-71; and: *Teaching International Business: Ethics and Corporate Social Responsibility* (ed: Gopalkrishnan R. Iyer) International Business Press, an imprint of The Haworth Press, Inc., 1999, pp. 43-71. Single or multiple copies of this article are available for a fee from The Haworth Document Delivery Service [1-800-342-9678, 9:00 a.m. - 5:00 p.m. (EST). E-mail address: getinfo@haworthpressinc.com].

43

perspectives to become better informed on the range of content and viewpoints on business ethics in an international environment. *[Article copies available for a fee from The Haworth Document Delivery Service: 1-800-342-9678. E-mail address: getinfo@haworthpressinc.com <Website: http://www.haworthpressinc.com>]*

KEYWORDS. International business ethics, disciplinary perspective, business curriculum, teaching ethics

INTRODUCTION

In a report on the international nature of the business ethics curriculum, Cowton and Dunfee (1995) concluded that most ethics educators believe "current teaching materials on the international dimension of business ethics fall far short of satisfactory" (pg. 334). The Cowton and Dunfee article called for the development of teaching materials that facilitate international concerns in the business ethics curriculum. Similarly, a perusal of international business texts reveals that very few have devoted significant space to ethics and ethical issues. Although the ethics component may be implicit in a discussion of international business strategy, this is anecdotal evidence that educators in international business need guidance on including ethics in the curriculum. Thus, there are a variety of impetuses for examining ethics in international business education.

In this paper, we discuss international ethics issues and perspectives from the vantage point of five disciplines in business education. The ethics of international business are examined from the economics, management, finance, accounting, and marketing traditions. Because of the differing natures of the disciplines and professors' functional graduate training, it is difficult for educators to master the ethical issues and perspectives of each functional area. This paper is a resource and guide for instructors facing the challenge of making the business curriculum more inclusive of ethical issues in an international context. Instead of debating broad philosophical beliefs, the paper takes a practical orientation for recognizing ethical issues in international business.

GENERAL TRENDS
IN INTERNATIONAL BUSINESS ETHICS

Although this paper is primarily focused on ethical issues in business functional areas, it is instructive to examine general trends in international business ethics and subsequent ramifications for business students and organizations. First, many organizations are joining alliances to support unilateral initiatives in the area of global compliance. Support for the requirements of the United States (U.S.) Foreign Corrupt Practices Act has come through a global treaty signed by 34 nations called the "Convention in Combating Bribery of Foreign Public Officials in International Business Transactions." The treaty requires those signing to make it a criminal offense for any person to "offer, promise, or give any undue pecuniary or other advantage . . . to a foreign public official," for the purpose of obtaining "business or other improper advantage in the conduct of international commerce." The punishment is to be determined by the country in which the company operates and should be effective in deterring future offenses (Kalthenhauser 1998). For example, the U.S. Senate confirmed the provisions of the treaty and appropriate sanctions in November 1998.

Second, the Caux Round Table Principles for Business represent a global effort at managing business ethics (http://astro.temple.edu/ ~ dialogue/Antho/caux_in.htm). The Caux Principles were developed by corporate representatives from multinational firms in Japan, Europe, and the United States, who wanted to establish a set of common values and expectations for business practice (Mankower 1994, Vega 1997). When corporations become signatories to the Caux Principles, they agree to uphold ethical standards relating to human rights, the physical environment, community participation, bribery and corruption, and many others. Alliances like the two mentioned above improve the ability of organizations to cooperate, negotiate, and navigate differences throughout the world. Because efforts on international business ethics and compliance have the potential to affect every role and department in business, students should be aware of them.

Finally, an important trend in international business ethics is toward the institutionalization of ethics and compliance programs (Thorne LeClair, Ferrell, and Ferrell, 1997). These programs, just like quality management initiatives, are designed for process and outcome improvements. In this case, the effort should create, reinforce, and sustain a corporate culture of integrity. As a result of the United States Federal Sentencing Guidelines for Organizations, Canada's Competition Act, the Australian Trade Practices Act, and similar measures in the European Union, most global organizations are aware of the key elements required to develop a successful ethical compliance program.

These include establishing a code of conduct, appointing a high level compliance manager, taking care in delegation of authority, instituting a training and communication system, monitoring and auditing for misconduct, enforcing and disciplining offenders, and revising the program as needed.

Under the federal regulation mentioned above, management assumes responsibility for developing and implementing "effective" ethical compliance programs. This means all managers and employees must understand the values, risks, and control mechanisms necessary to create an ethical culture. Under this rubric, corporate strategy and activities must be consistent with expectations for legal and ethical conduct. With the structural elements of an ethical compliance program generally agreed upon, an important step is to address the issues involved in developing the global program. For the purpose of this paper, students need to understand specific ethical issues in order to manage for ethical decision-making in the international environment.

Functional specialists will experience ethical dilemmas that are embedded in their daily activities. For example, a marketing manager may discover the unwritten rules of exporting and importing when she encounters a corrupt customs official. Or, a purchasing manager may be shocked when he learns that a vendor is using child labor. In both cases, the ethical issue emerged through the process of daily responsibilities. However, this does not suggest that ethical issues are isolated as the sole concern of specific departments. On the contrary, ethical dilemmas experienced in functional areas should be viewed as organizational issues that require strategic reflection and direction. Based on ethical problems and other influences, the ethical compliance program would be continuously improved to anticipate and negate future ethical issues.

To facilitate the discussion of ethical issues in different roles and functions, each section below presents an overview of the opportunity for international ethics education in a particular academic area. An underlying theme is the challenge of organizing and controlling business behavior in an increasingly interconnected and complex world. Managing for productive and ethical decisions is difficult enough in a homogeneous world. But as each of the following sections illustrate, the challenges are exacerbated due to powerful differences in business environments.

ECONOMICS

Economics' underlying principles continue to inform modern accounting, finance, marketing, and management. Although most business organizations do not have an economics department, the academic discipline is considered fundamental to an understanding of effective business practice. To this end, most business students must complete principles courses in microeconomics and macroeconomics. The overall goal in these courses is typically to provide a foundation for understanding the economic environment of business. Because additional economics study (beyond principles) is most often not required of undergraduate business students, this section will focus on opportunities to provide exposure to principles level economics. The international ethics content, as based on economics principles courses, can be used in a variety of upper level business classes.

Internationalizing Principles of Economics

Joseph Stiglitz (1993) writes that, "providing an international perspective not only can enrich the standard course, but beyond that, is necessary if we are to understand modern economics, in all of its manifestations." Both microeconomics and macroeconomics provide opportunities to introduce basic concepts in international economics. Topics in international economics include comparative advantage, multinational corporations, trade policy, trade balance, foreign investment, exchange rates, twin deficits, world monetary systems, and world banking systems. Of course, it is very important to provide all business students with an introduction to these topics, which are international by definition.

Another approach suggests that global perspectives are also necessary in order to reach correct conclusions using economic theory and discussing economic policy. For instance, when discussing market structure and antitrust issues, professors and students may understate the level of competitiveness by limiting the analysis to domestic firms. Or they might assume that a monetary expansion will necessarily increase investment (as it does in a closed economy). An examination of domestic automobile production and labor issues cannot be complete without fully considering the role of foreign suppliers.

Gordon (1993) suggests that students can also benefit from what he calls "comparative economics." He states, "comparative economics examines differences in economic behavior across space and time both to illustrate economic theories and to question their validity" (p. 17). Comparative economics assesses whether "economic success is a matter of following basic economic principles, or whether culture, institutions, and attitudes also play a role" (p. 18). Gordon's approach opens traditional principles topics up to deeper examination across political and geographic boundaries.

Ethics and Economic Principles

According to most that have studied business curriculum, economists have contributed little to the ethics education of business students. In a study by Pizzolatto and Bevill (1996), economics was last in the percentage of undergraduate students reporting at least one class session devoted to the topic. Furthermore, over half the student respondents said they did not recall or there was no class discussion of ethics in their finance and economics courses. A casual survey of principles of microeconomics and managerial economics textbooks (undergraduate and graduate) reveals little coverage of ethics. It seems as though economics has room to increase its participation in the ethics education of business students.[1]

Principles courses typically include a careful presentation of the difference between positive economics and normative economics. Most caution students that economic science is concerned with positive questions. To some, a concern for ethics issues conflicts with the goal of getting students to "think like an economist." Others disagree. Hausman and McPherson (1993, p. 673) argue that there are at least four reasons why economists should care about ethics:

1. The morality of economic agents influences their behavior and hence influences economic outcomes. Moreover, economists' own moral views may influence the morality and the behavior of others in both intended and unintended ways. Because economists are interested in the outcomes, they must be interested in morality.

2. Standard welfare economics rests on strong and contestable moral presuppositions. To assess and to develop welfare economics thus requires attention to morality.

3. The conclusions of economics must be linked to the moral commitments that drive public policy. To understand how economics

bears on policy thus requires that one understand these moral commitments, which in turn requires attentions to morality.

4. Positive and normative economics are frequently intermingled. To understand the moral relevance of positive economics requires an understanding of the moral principles that determine this relevance.

With regard to the contributions of economics to the international business ethics, the first of the four reasons seems the most relevant.[2] It is easy to demonstrate that morality affects economic transactions and efficiency in economic systems. For example, when simple assumptions about information are relaxed, equilibrium outcomes in market systems may no longer be efficient. To illustrate, the market for good used cars may be smaller (than is efficient) due to the fact that sellers have better information about the quality of their cars than do buyers. The source of this problem is not just the asymmetry in information, but also that sellers of "lemons" may be dishonest to prospective buyers. Most economists tend to focus on market responses to this problem (e.g., private warranties, inspection, reputation, etc . . .) than the obvious ethical issue. In a related example, it is often not possible to effectively monitor the behavior of employees. The result may be employee theft, poor customer relations, lower quality, and related problems. Most economists know these problems as "adverse selection" and "agency problems," respectively. Other business professors know them as important ethical issues.

Incentives: Ethics and Comparative Economics

There are many opportunities to internationalize basic economics principles (e.g., international economics, comparative economic systems, and comparative economics). Similarly, ethics could reveal itself in economics in a variety of ways (e.g., welfare analysis, informational problems, etc.). A natural intersection between global issues and ethics occurs under the broad category of "incentives." A discussion of incentives provides an excellent opportunity to apply Gordon's comparative economics approach while developing a solid foundation for understanding ethical decision making from an economics perspective.

The study of incentives, of course, consumes economics and may be discussed in a variety of contexts (i.e., markets and organizations) and levels (i.e., macro and micro). Ubiquitous and richly complex, incentive problems are created when goals and objectives conflict in economic relationships and transactions. Incentives are influenced by economic institutions, which differ across political and cultural boundaries. Although it is not possible to present an exhaustive list of examples, a few are described below. The ethical issues should be obvious in each case:

> Perhaps the most obvious example concerns the role of markets and prices. In some countries, output and prices in many industries are controlled by government planners. Unfortunately, when held too low (as they often are) a black market will likely develop. This activity (illegal in most countries) is often run "on the side" by employees of legitimate businesses selling the product.

> Health care systems create different incentives in the United States than they do in Canada. With fee-for-service, surgeons in the United States may be tempted to conduct unnecessary procedures. In Canada, patients may have an incentive to offer bribes to move quickly to the front of the queue.

> In order to meet production goals, workers in the former Soviet Union may have incentives to sacrifice quality. In the United States, there may be similar outcomes as some workers respond to piece-rate compensation plans.

> In *Principles of Macroeconomics*, N. Gregory Mankiw uses a *New York Times* article written by Peter Passell to discuss the Laffer curve. In the Ukraine's post-Communist economy, the high tax rate and burdensome regulations provided tremendous incentive to operate illegitimate businesses. According to one estimate cited in the article, the "unofficial" economy was bigger than the "official" economy in 1996. (Mankiw 1998, p. 169)

Using the comparative economics approach, the questions in these cases relate to whether the observed behavior is consistent with economic models: Are there historical or cultural differences that explain inconsistencies with the theories? Some students at Harvard want to explore the political and social issues that affect economic theory. Calling themselves SHARE (Students for Humane and Responsible Economics), the students are urging professors of introductory economics to provide alternative explanations for traditional economic assumptions (Anonymous 1998a). By examining the incentives created by economic systems and comparing them across cultures, economists not only take business students a long way towards understanding the challenges associated with international business ethics, they also provide a richer understanding of economic theory.

FINANCE

The financial challenges of operating in international markets are evident when considering the regulatory risks in developing entrance and exit strategies for overseas investments. A key issue in addressing these risks is the identification and implementation of ethical standards. In the absence of defined and enforceable ethical standards of business practice, international firms (and individuals) may find themselves operating in environments where the legal and ethical standards of business are lower in the host country than in their home country. This point should be communicated to students, who may be less aware of these effects on financial decision making.

Firms that operate in an environment where management exercises a fiduciary duty based on the property rights of shareholders implement ethics codes as part of a strategy to maximize shareholder wealth. Thus, fiduciary duties are founded primarily on the needs of the owner to restrain managerial discretion as in a classic agency problem. For example, managers may have different objectives (e.g., maximizing short-term profits) than shareholders (e.g., maximizing the value of the firm), which can lead to ethical dilemmas.

The financial challenges in dealing with the ethics issue is the difficulty in clearly identifying the net present value factors when the proposed standards are beyond those legally required. An example would be the firm's use of child labor. While various nations may view the use of child labor as a cultural norm, an international firm may elect to recognize the importance of raising its own standards in those markets. This decision, while increasing labor costs, may contribute to a significantly enhanced corporate image, however providing quantification to cost benefits of the policy may prove difficult. Nike's recent decision to increase the standards of its international labor practices may be a case in point.

The challenge for shareholders is made more difficult by the firm's interpretation of its ethical environment. Is the standard to be observed a regulatory standard fixed by government regulation, or is it subject to judicial interpretation? The central aim of financial regulation is to ensure the equitable treatment of all corporate constituencies. However, often U.S. firms confront a double standard overseas. For example, U.S. businesses are subject to the legal requirements of the Foreign Corrupt Practices Act, which prohibits American companies from bribing foreign officials to obtain business. However, despite legal restrictions in overseas markets prohibiting this behavior the difference between observed and required ethical behavior leaves a great deal of interpretation. As an example, in January 1998 the Tokyo Prosecutor's Office raided the Ministry of Finance (MOF) resulting in the subsequent arrest of two Banking Bureau officials on charges of accepting bribes from commercial banks. This precipitated a series of top-level resignations, as well as the suicide of a third examiner (Wanner 1998). In creating a regulatory environment that lacked clear guidelines Japanese bureaucrats had given themselves great discretion in implementing laws and regulations and consequently increased their power. Through this power they fostered a lack of transparency between agencies and their regulators. This situation created a competitive disadvantage for foreign firms seeking to conduct business in the Japanese market.

A company's standards should be summarized in a written code of conduct that is strictly enforced. In the case of foreign subsidiaries or contractors, the document should be translated into the local language and adapted to address international business issues. A critical factor in the development and implementation of an international code of ethics is the company's motivation. If the company's management implements an ethics code because it believes in the appropriateness of the guidelines, the code will be significantly stronger than if they merely consider the financial consequences of avoiding lawsuits or minimizing damages if sued. For example, Daiwa Bank of Japan was permanently barred from conducting business in the United States because the company was slow to respond to Securities and Exchange Commission (SEC) rules on reporting financial losses and employee misconduct. Essentially, top executives at Daiwa were torn between SEC rules and the wishes of Japan's Ministry of Finance to keep the losses private for a certain time period. Daiwa's punishment was only exacerbated by the lack of an effective ethical compliance program (Thorne LeClair, Ferrell and Ferrell 1997).

Individual versus Corporate Responsibility

In addition to standards at the corporate level, international financial markets pose significant ethical challenges to individual market participants. Due to differences in business cultures, international investors have found it difficult to develop and enforce consistent global standards. An illustration of the difficulty in establishing international standards for financial practice is the global treatment of insider securities trading. After the recent adoption of insider trading regulations by German securities markets, all major and emerging international securities markets make insider-trading illegal. However, in the U.S. the specific application of insider trading rules (it is illegal) have been developed through judicial interpretation. In many emerging markets, despite government regulation of insider trading (it is illegal), there are few, if any case law applications of the legal code to practice, even in markets where the practice is common.

Enforcement of insider trading rules is a challenge in every market. Thus, although insider trading is common in many emerging markets it is not prosecuted for fear of damaging market liquidity. Stiff penalties are required for traders to take the regulations seriously. For example, in Canada the penalty for illegal insider trading is up to two years in prison and the greater of $1 million or three times the profit made from the trade.

The problem is perennial in financial regulation: how to crack down on abusive practices–price manipulation, insider trading and the like . . . The UK government's answer is to give strong and flexible powers to its new regulator, the Financial Services Authority, balanced by appeals to an independent tribunal. Like the Securities and Exchange Commission in the U.S., the FSA is to be given the power to impose civil sanctions, including unlimited fines. Legislation will set out very generally what constitutes unacceptable behaviour, while the FSA will issue a much more detailed-and amendable-code of conduct. A first draft of the code has just been issued for comment. Both the government's broad architecture and the FSA code deserve qualified support. For the existing statutory framework, enshrined in the 1986 Financial Services Act and the 1993 Criminal Justice Act, has not proved particularly effective. (Anonymous 1998b)

This British legislation marks the first time that the chief regulator in Britain is provided with the power to prosecute cases of insider dealing, market manipulation, and money laundering (Jones 1998). Market regulators contend that in developing securities markets they must develop a body of law. The second step is actual enforcement.

Code of Ethics for International Finance

To create a more equitable trading environment, efforts have been underway to develop an appropriate ethical code for international investors. In the U.S. the Association for Investment Management and Research (AIMR) has been in the forefront of developing appropriate standards for investment managers and for the presentation of their performance:

> The AIMR Performance Presentation Standards were first introduced by the Financial Analysts Federation's Committee for Performance Presentation Standards (PPS) in the September/October 1987 issue of the *Financial Analysts Journal*. Since that time, the AIMR-PPS standards have been reviewed extensively by members of the industry and revised in response to their many comments and recommendations. (Association for Investment Management and Research 1997)

In 1990, the AIMR Board of Governors endorsed the AIMR-PPS standards and approved the establishment of the Performance Presentation Standards Implementation Committee to review the Standards and seek industry input prior to formal implementation in 1993. The Implementation Committee continues to operate as a standing AIMR committee with the responsibilities of reviewing the Standards as the industry evolves, providing interpretation and clarification of the Standards, and expanding the principles of the Standards as new situations warrant. In 1995, AIMR formed the Global PPS Subcommittee to further address international performance issues and to develop global standards for presenting investment performance. Outside North America, the Swiss Bankers Association has adopted standards virtually identical to the AIMR-PPS standards.

The ethical standards for a Chartered Financial Analyst (CFA) clearly state that when the host nation's standards hold an investment advisor to a lower standard of conduct, the AIMR standards are effective (i.e., even if a nation permits insider trading it is restricted for a CFA charter holder and candidate.) This standardization is essential to even the playing field and reduce the incentives for unethical behavior.

International securities market regulators are taking the lead not only in Britain with the new Financial Services Authority, but also in articulating a Code of Ethics for market participants. An example of this is the Securities Institute of Australia's Code of Ethics (http://securities.edu.au/code.htm). Regulatory standardization will reduce the challenge to corporate and individual financial market participants over their ethical standards. However, the lack of an international regulatory authority will still leave actual compliance to the organization or individual. These complexities should be properly integrated into a discussion of international (and domestic) finance.

ACCOUNTING

Accounting practices originally developed to satisfy domestic information needs. Consequently, accounting standards in different nations took on characteristics that reflected the differences in culture that directed the ways businesses were organized, financed and controlled in distinctively different nations. In an environment of truly global financial markets, there is a pressing need for investors anywhere in the world to be able read, interpret, evaluate, and compare financial statements from firms located virtually everywhere. To enable firms to list their stocks on worldwide stock exchanges, there must be essential commonality in the way firms disclose information about the results of their operations. There are currently efforts to "harmonize" accounting standards between nations.

Common auditing standards are just as important as common accounting standards. The readers of financial statements rely on the attestations made by auditors as to the fairness of the financial representation. When auditing standards differ, or the qualifications to become an auditor vary greatly between nations (even if the financial statements were prepared under identical accounting standards), then the credibility of financial reporting is brought into question.

Ethics are culturally based, drawing on legal standards, societal norms, domestic religious convictions, and other institutions. Cultural forces underlie the development of accounting and auditing standards or the willingness to accept an international set of standards. Different cultures (i.e., different standards of ethics) drive what is appropriate to disclose in financial statements and the obligations of auditors to report on their findings. Because of the momentum to harmonize generally accepted accounting principles (GAAP) worldwide, the accounting discipline has attempted to categorize differences in culture that might affect accounting practice.

Culture-Based Differences

Much international business literature concerns the grouping of nations into cultural categories based on five major distinctions developed by Hofstede (1980). These categories include: (1) Large power distance versus small power distance, (2) Individualism versus collectivism, (3) Long-term versus short-term orientation, (4) Uncertainty avoidance versus uncertainty acceptance, and (5) High masculinity versus low masculinity. Hofstede's work is often cited in the international business literature and has been applied in the accounting discipline as well.

A full treatise on these five distinctions is beyond the scope of this brief overview (for more information, please reference Hofstede 1980 and Hofstede and Bond 1984). However, accounting researchers have placed different nations into categories based on these distinctions and have explained the degree to which individual nations might require financial disclosures and the degree to which an auditor within that nation might be willing to reveal audit findings.

Cultural Effects on Generally Accepted Accounting Principles (GAAP)

Because of differences in these cultural characteristics, the manner in which GAAP is established and the latitude offered under the standards will differ between nations. Table 1 shows how these cultural distinctions may affect GAAP (Haskins, Ferris and Selling 1996; Zarzeski 1996a).

What is considered ethical in terms of financial reporting depends on the cultural distinctions that helped establish the set of ethical standards. For example, high power distance cultures see nothing unethical in limiting financial disclosure (i.e., maintaining secrecy about the results of operations) because this restricts information and

TABLE 1. How Cultural Distinctions Affect Generally Accepted Accounting Principles

Cultural Distinction	High Value	Low Value
Power Distance	Statutory control of GAAP. Uniformity in reporting. Less financial disclosure.	Professional control of GAAP. Flexibility in reporting. Greater financial disclosure
Individualism	Professional control of GAAP. Flexibility in reporting. Greater financial disclosure. Less conservative accounting.	Statutory control of GAAP. Uniformity in reporting. Less financial disclosure. More conservative accounting.
Long-Term Orientation	Uniformity in reporting. More conservative accounting	Flexibility in reporting. Less conservative accounting.
Uncertainty Avoidance	Uniformity in reporting. Less financial disclosure. More conservative accounting More rules and preference for international harmonization.	Flexibility in reporting. Greater financial disclosure. Less conservative accounting. Less rules and less concern for international harmonization.
Masculinity	Greater financial disclosure.	Less financial disclosure.

preserves power and role inequalities. In general, research indicates that the secretiveness of a culture does underlie disclosure practices of its business enterprises (Zarzeski 1996b). Within those societies, that is seen as normal. These cultural distinctions are by no means the only forces influencing GAAP, however, several studies have demonstrated consistent results.

For example, in Islamic societies, it is unethical and contrary to religious belief to use interest or interest-bearing financial instruments (Hamid, Craig and Clarke 1993). Such nations would never accept accounting principles based on present value (i.e., the time value of money concept). Thus, Western standards for valuing long-term debt instruments or capital leases are unacceptable in Islamic societies. How does one harmonize accounting standards globally when faced with deep religious ethical rules or societal ethical standards that are so important to a culture? Nations with fundamental ethical differences may still find it necessary to adopt international accounting standards in order to raise financing. There is evidence that financing needs and other market forces affect disclosure behavior (Zarzeski 1996b). To accomplish their international goals, firms from cultures that ethically reject Western accounting standards will most likely maintain double accounting standards–one for reporting within the nation, and another for purposes of listing stocks on international stock markets and conducting international commerce. These double standards are used in Islamic societies, China, and elsewhere (Adhikari and Wang 1995; Winkle, Huss and Xi-Zhu 1994). Students of accounting need to know that GAAP is not just what is taught in their universities. National differences in accepted accounting standards exist because of differences in ethical standards, industry regulation, and general cultural beliefs.

Cultural Effects on Generally Accepted Auditing Standards (GAAS)

Just as GAAP differs due to cultural distinctions in ethical standards, more so does the role of the "independent" auditor who audits the financial statements of a firm. Table 2 shows how the auditor may be affected based on the cultural distinctions exhibited by the country (Cohen, Pant and Sharp 1993; Johnson 1992).

Some societies, particularly African and Asian, exhibit high power distance, collectivism (i.e., low individualism), long-term orientation, and high uncertainty avoidance. In those societies, the independence of the auditor from the client might be questioned. Auditors in such societies may act in a manner that in the United States (U.S.) would be considered highly unethical. That is, the auditor may acquiesce to the client, not probe as deeply, be more tolerant of accounting manipulation, fail to report findings, and be protective of the client who is being audited. Many such countries also exhibit low masculinity. They would quickly dismiss the opinion of a female auditor who attempts to act ethically and report inappropriate client behavior. Accounting students need to be aware that ethical implications and pressures will differ greatly depending on the society in which the auditor practices.

MARKETING

The functional area of marketing has received a great deal of criticism for personal selling, advertising practices, fraudulent marketing

TABLE 2. How Cultural Distinctions Affect Generally Accepted Auditing Standards

Cultural Distinction	High Value	Low Value
Power Distance	Difficult to resist pressure from wealthy/powerful clients. May acquiesce to superior's request to underreport or underperform audit work. If auditor feels ethically obligated to be independent, may resort to "secret audits," remain aloof from client, find all mistakes, adversely affects professionalism.	Less intimated and can be more independent from client who pays them. More insistent that proper accounting be performed.
Individualism	Speaking your mind is a virtue. Auditor is more independent from client. It is expected to identify client weaknesses in accounting or control.	It is rude to confront others. Auditor must still protect the group from outsiders. It is insulting to identify client weaknesses in accounting or control. Only "loyal" auditors have career potential, adversely affects professionalism.
Long-Term Orientation	Willingness to subordinate oneself to the group may influence depth of inspection or honesty of the audit report.	Over-aggressively solicit clients who may be risky. Cut audit work to achieve billable hour projections. Underreport actual audit hours to stay within projections.
Uncertainty Avoidance	If it's legal then it's ethical and absence of a disallowing rule makes client's action okay. Focus on form of an issue versus contents. More easily accepts client's accounting.	Absence of a disallowing rule creates greater dependence on auditor judgment. Focus on content of an issue versus form. Will take issue with client's accounting.
Masculinity	Female auditor opinions are equally respected/accepted. Female auditors are more likely to act unethically for self-interest.	Female auditor opinions are less respected/accepted Female auditors are less likely to act unethically for self-interest.

research and a number of other marketing activities (Goolsby and Hunt 1992; Murphy and Laczniak 1981). Researchers in marketing ethics have responded to such criticism by developing theory and conducting empirical studies on ethical decision making. In addition, most professional marketing associations have detailed codes of ethics, including the American Marketing Association (http://207. 154.156.75/about/ama/fulleth.asp), Direct Marketing Association (http://www.the-dma.org), Marketing Research Association (http:// www.mra-net.org/MEMBERSHIP/codestand.html), and European Society for Opinion and Marketing Research (http://www.esomar.nl/ codes_and_guidelines.html).

Research in Marketing Ethics

Since the mid-1980s, researchers in marketing ethics have developed several positive or descriptive models of ethical decision making (e.g., Ferrell and Gresham 1985; Hunt and Vitell 1986). These models delineate the major influences on (un)ethical decisions and focus on describing the process of decision making. The models' authors do not make any normative statements about what is right or wrong in marketing activities. Rather, they describe the characteristics of individuals and organizations that affect the ethical decision making process. Simplified versions of these marketing ethics models are used in some Principles of Marketing textbooks. These textbooks include marketing ethics as either a standalone chapter or integrated into concept areas. Although ethical decision-making has become a viable, relevant and popular topic of study in the marketing discipline, there is less evidence that this focus has fully filtered into classroom activities, especially with an international perspective. For example, in a study by Shannon and Berl (1997), students rated the discussion of ethics in the international marketing course was somewhere between "weak" and "adequate." Shannon and Berl (1997) state:

> With the varying ethical standards found in foreign cultures and the impact of these standards on business practices, it would have been expected that there would have been a higher level of discussion of ethics in (international marketing) courses. (pg. 1065)

Ethical Issues in International Marketing

It is clear that students (and instructors) need guidance on ethical issues in international marketing. Ethical issues that arise in an international context can be very similar to those found in the domestic environment. Other ethical dilemmas are the direct result of variations in law and expectations for the conduct of business. To prevent these occurrences, it is incumbent on marketing managers and employees to understand the legal and ethical standards that affect marketing strategy development and implementation. Just as an understanding of culture will lead to more effective product design and strategy, it can also protect an organization from mistakes and violations that detract from marketing and business performance. Thus, ethical issues in the international environment should not be treated in isolation from other marketing processes and decisions. This suggests that marketing educators should integrate ethics into all aspects of marketing planning and execution (e.g., product development, pricing decisions, advertising platform). Further, marketers must have a system for recognizing and responding to unique legal systems, ethical values, and cultural nuances. This system begins with a fundamental analysis of risk areas within marketing decision-making. The issues discussed below are organized along the fundamental aspects of marketing strategy and are designed for classroom use.

Product. As the foundational element of marketing strategy, a product must be designed to meet customer needs in an ethical and legal manner. However, because of variances in laws and other norms, ethical issues can emerge in the global arena. One common concern is the sale of harmful products in other countries. In this case, products may have been banned by a firm's domestic government but not in other countries. The firm may then decide to market the product, now considered harmful, in nations without the regulation. A classic example of this situation is with the chemical, DDT, that was banned in the U.S. in the early 1970s but continued to be marketed in developing countries (Fritzsche 1985). Other ethical issues in product management relate to environmental effects, such as pollution, deforestation, and the protection of natural assets. Again, regulatory variance may permit specific actions in one country, but not another. Finally, there are some products that a segment of the population will consider harmful, even if governments have not outlawed their sale and use (i.e., tobacco, alcohol). In this case, however, there may be stringent controls on the pricing, promotion, and distribution of these products.

Pricing. A common pricing issue in international marketing is "dumping." Dumping is the practice of selling products in other countries for a price below production costs. This practice may be seen as an appropriate strategy for generating market share and presence, but is highly questionable in most legal and ethical contexts. A recent example of an international pricing issue is found in an article by Thorne LeClair, Ferrell and Ferrell (1997):

> It has been alleged that NEC Corporation attempted to sell super-computers to the National Science Foundation (NSF) below competitors' prices. The Commerce Department informed the foundation that the offer did not constitute the fair market value of the products, alluding to dumping activities. The International Fair Competition Act of 1992 makes it clear that unfair foreign competition that occurs in the U.S. domestic market does not have to demonstrate intent–only that unfair foreign competition occurred.

Distribution. A fundamental distribution question facing international marketers is the payment of bribes to facilitate distribution and transportation in a country. The documentation and approval process accompanying imports to a country may be coupled with the expectation of a facilitating payment or bribe. In addition, other aspects of distribution and production may be subject to such payments. For example, Del Monte Corporation paid nearly $500,000 to a "banana consultant" to assist with the purchase of a banana plantation in Guatemala. Del Monte's request to purchase the plantation had been repeatedly denied by the Guatemalan government. However, the government reversed its decision after the company paid the consultant (Fritzsche 1985).

Promotion. As the communication element of the marketing mix, promotional strategy is subject to interpretations that must pass both legal and ethical standards. Because of the interpretive and perceptual element of communications, international marketers must be extremely careful in developing promotional strategy. There are many examples of promotional words and symbols that, when translated or used in another culture, have created embarrassing marketing situations.

Other examples in the promotion area include:

1. Companies entering Saudi Arabia may not be aware that the sales profession is not held in high regard. Thus, a company accustomed to designing marketing strategy with a heavy sales force component will need to reconsider this strategy in Saudi Arabia.
2. Mitsubishi misjudged the United States legal system in a public relations strategy designed to influence public and government opinion about a sexual harassment lawsuit. On company time, 3000 Mitsubishi employees attended a rally to protest the lawsuit. The rally only infuriated many constituents.
3. The European Economic Community recently issued directives on many sales techniques, including telemarketing, mail order, and direct television sales. These directives are designed to protect consumer rights and are more strict than many national laws (Gabbott 1994).

Customer Orientation and Marketing Concept

Finally, it is also important to communicate with students on the nature of the marketing concept. Once an organization decides to make customer satisfaction, not just profitability, a core objective then a relationship orientation has been established. When organizations begin to focus on customer relationships and the development of trust, the language and promise of ethics has been employed. If the company is truly customer-centered, then a marketing strategy that deceives or gouges will not be tolerated. Thus, as marketing continues to mature, its core concepts and practices will also evolve with respect to an ethical orientation. Many organizations are aware of the linkage between business ethics and long-term performance (i.e., stronger employee commitment, better customer satisfaction, fewer regulatory problems). This linkage can also be made in the international business environment.

MANAGEMENT

In many colleges, the management department has assumed primary responsibility for teaching business ethics and business and society-related topics and courses. The management discipline has an academic tradition of examining how organizations can manage and lead for ethical decision making (e.g., Jones 1991). This section extends this tradition by examining concepts and recent examples that illustrate the management of business ethics in a global environment.

One key mistake that many companies (and students) make is to assume that their home country values, with respect to ethical and legal issues, are universal. For example, the U.S. has a strong compliance or legal orientation. Therefore, in expanding operations globally, U.S. firms assume a legal orientation to be the norm. In other countries and cultures, certain laws are often interpreted more situationally or within specific contexts and are either accepted or ignored based on the economic environment or the rewards offered by business to the community or country.

Ethical Issues in International Management

Key issues that must be considered from a management perspective include organizing, directing, planning, and controlling employees' activities. Since managers guide employee behaviors, they influence the ethical culture of the organization. Human resource issues are a concern for managers, including areas such as hiring, employee discipline, discrimination, health and safety, privacy, employee benefits, drug and alcohol abuse, plant closings, and layoffs. These issues may be handled through isolated decisions, but often have broader social and ethical ramifications. For example, a Nike subcontractor in Vietnam was accused of abusing employees, paying low wages, and enforcing long work periods without breaks. After much public criticism, Nike responded by placing corporate representatives within the manufacturing facilities to monitor and enforce certain workplace standards for the benefit of employees (Kish 1998). Managers, regardless of their functional responsibilities and country location, must be trained and motivated to recognize and respond appropriately to ethical issues. Important ethical issues for all employees and managers are explained in the following paragraphs.

Discrimination. Sexual and racial discrimination are issues of great importance in the U.S., but other countries deal with these issues differently. In Japan, females are rarely promoted to high positions within the organization and are generally subservient to males in business settings. Japan has made sex discrimination illegal, but it continues due to the lack of any penalty for violation. Middle Eastern countries only allow women to function in a non-business capacity. Female salespeople doing business in the Middle East have significantly less success and respect than males. Understanding the prevailing norms of a country will improve the chances of making the right decision with respect to key human rights issues.

Human Rights. Companies also face concerns related to minorities, child labor, women, and employees' rights. Global firms have a significant challenge because of the diverse laws and customs influencing their operations and subcontractor's operations throughout the world. The law in each country should be viewed as the floor of acceptable behavior. Some companies are increasingly taking responsibility for all stakeholder concerns and create checks and balances to prevent abuse. Levi Strauss & Company was the first multinational corporation to discuss human rights in its code of conduct. The Gap hired an independent agent to monitor its plants in San Salvador after accusations of human rights abuses (Kish 1998). Amnesty International is also helpful to multinational corporations (MNCs) on human rights issues in various countries.

A study conducted by the National Labor Committee found that American businesses are actually lowering the wages, benefits, and quality of work life for some Chinese employees. Sweatshops are widespread throughout China and many MNCs purchase products from these firms. At a Liang Shi handbag factory, workers make 13 cents per hour while a subsistence wage would be 87 cents per hour. The goods manufactured at this sweatshop were made available through WalMart under the Kathy Lee Gifford name (Anonymous 1998c).

Bribery and Corruption. Bribery has been a difficult issue for MNCs to deal with abroad. Many MNCs have been fined under the Foreign Corrupt Practices Act (FCPA) because of international bribery and corruption charges. Companies can receive fines up to $2 million or up to twice the values of the gain realized. Some U.S. business people have complained that FCPA restrictions make it very difficult to conduct business in some countries. For example, firms doing business in Indonesia must be aware that civil servants salaries are very low and that for them to make a livable wage, bribery is encouraged (Shari and Einhorn 1998). When doing business in the Ukraine, manufacturers and importers have many barriers to overcome before gaining entry into the market. Before a product is made available, it must be inspected by a team of government officials at the factory where it is manufactured. The manufacturer must pay the travel expenses of the team, plus up to $10,000 per visit. Products must be inspected or "reapproved" every two years. A World Bank survey of companies importing to the country found that 71 percent paid bribes to government officials (Matlack 1998).

To gain a broad understanding of the culture of a country, instructors and students can consult Transparency International to see the how countries rank in terms of corruptness (http:www.transparency.de). The 1998 survey showed Denmark, Finland, Sweden, New Zealand, Iceland, Canada, Switzerland, Netherlands, Norway, and Singapore as the least corrupt countries. Nigeria, Cameroon, Paraguay, Colombia, Russia, Indonesia, Venezuela, Honduras, Tanzania, and Ecuador were among the most corrupt countries (Transparency International 1998). Having a general understanding of the overall cultural orientation of the country can be helpful in assessing expansion of manufacturing or sales initiatives worldwide.

Power and Control of Multinational Corporations

Because of the size and inherent power of multinational corporations (MNCs), decisions made can have far reaching implications. The world's 500 largest industrial corporations employ just .05 of 1 percent of the world's population, yet control 25 percent of the world's economic output. More than 20 companies have an economic value greater than the Gross Domestic Product (GDP) of Hungary, Ireland, and Venezuela (Browne 1998). Due to the economic size and power of MNCs they are hard to monitor and influence, therefore, the control and reporting dimension of the management process becomes even more important in managing community and governmental relations. Although businesses of all sizes are concerned with control and enforceability, the sheer size and dispersion of MNC operations create unique challenges.

Decentralization is a key issue for MNCs, since company representation and activities extend to countries with varying laws and ethical expectations. For example, Texas Instruments has taken great strides to implement company-wide values that are applicable in all locations and operations (http://www.ti.com). Multinational corporations face extreme complexity in managing many employees, who are working in countries with different legal and ethical systems. For example, IBM's reputation has been tarnished in Argentina by allegations that it provided kickbacks to government officials in order to obtain a $249 million dollar contract to computerize the state owned Banco Nacion. IBM, indicating knowledge of the kickback, will have four employees testify under the bilateral U.S.-Argentine Treaty. If the allegations are found to be true, IBM would be subject to prosecution under the Foreign Corrupt Practices Act (Associated Press 1998).

TEACHING APPLICATION AND CONCLUSION

In this paper, we have examined key ethical issues and perspectives in five disciplines in business education. Educators teaching international business courses need to have knowledge about each of the main business functions. This expertise includes an understanding of ethical issues and perspectives, which involves business practice, cultural expectations, legal systems and other parts of economic institutions and society. By the same token, ethics educators need an awareness of the unique ethical issues that arise in international business practice. This article is designed as a collection of perspectives for educating students on ethics in international economics, management, marketing, accounting, and finance. The underlying theme on all dimensions is management awareness, accountability, and control for ethical decision-making. Ethical issues often arise from daily actions and when not properly managed, become larger issues to be dealt with by society, government, and other institutions.

Although there has been some debate over whether ethics can be taught (e.g., Bok 1976), the perspective taken in this article is one of creating awareness of ethical issues. With undergraduate students, a key pedagogical barrier can be students' lack of work experience. In this case, the instructor will need to provide more detail on the day-to-day realities that can create ethical conflict. Pressure to meet deadlines and objectives, interpersonal relationships and conflict, competitive threats, governmental intervention, and other factors affect business ethical decision-making. When presenting and discussing international business ethics, instructors can draw on the same pedagogical tools used for other subjects. International business ethics and related concepts can be taught and learned via lecture, case discussion, role-play, and other mechanisms. However, pedagogy that embraces active learning, debate, reasoning, and a practical orientation will likely be more effective (Glass and Bonnici 1997).

For example, the following ethics-related projects can be easily implemented in courses on international business and functional areas:

> International marketing students role-play a sales negotiation situation involving companies from countries with different laws and expectations regarding facilitating payments, environmental regulations or other sensitive matters.

> International finance and accounting students research the certification process for professionals in three countries and then report on any differences. The report should also examine codes of ethics and other standards that affect professionals' work activities (e.g., independence roles governing the audit/client relationship).

> International economics students communicate with students in countries at different stages of economic development to examine the effects of public policy on legal and ethical expectations for business conduct. Students may also communicate with students in countries of similar economic development to examine these expectations.

> International management students complete a country profile that includes a review of existing business practices and standards, with commentary on how these standards are similar or different from their home country.

> International business students develop an ethics audit of a multinational corporation by reviewing its code of ethics, mission and vision statement, company policies, and related information.

This paper has presented ethical issues that can be integrated into the international business curriculum. While not exhaustive, these issues provide instructors with material on which to base ethics discussions and class projects. There are many opportunities for theory and curricular advances in this area. Future research may focus on developing an overarching framework for leveraging functional perspectives to enhance international business ethics education. Other authors may build on the ideas to develop experiential classroom exercises. Finally, we hope this paper will spark continued debate and discussion regarding the intersection of ethics and international business.

NOTES

1. Economists have contributed to the coverage of ethics in the business curriculum in other ways. In fact, in a study conducted by Collins and Wartick (1995), economists represent eleven percent of full-time instructors teaching societal issues courses. The same study indicates that in 1990, twenty-eight percent of the surveyed schools have at least one business and society instructor from the economics area. In addition, economists have recently published books with titles that include words like *Ethics*, *Trust*, *Social Contract*, *Altruism*, and *Credibility*. At least one new managerial economics textbook dedicates a whole chapter to ethics.

2. This does not mean that the other three are less important. In fact, many would argue that the strongest contribution that economists can make is to prepare students who understand the moral foundations of welfare analysis and policy choice (both topics in principles of economics).

REFERENCES

Adhikar, A. and Wang, S.Z. (1995). Accounting for China, *Management Accounting* (April), 27-32.

Anonymous (1998a). Dueling Handouts: Harvard Students Challenge Economic Orthodoxy, *Business Ethics* (November/December), 6.

Anonymous (1998b). City regulation. *Financial Times (London)*, (June 30), 21.

Anonymous (1998c). American Companies are Actually Lowering Labor Standards in China, *Business Ethics* (May/June), 9.

Association for Investment Management and Research (1997). *AIMR Performance Presentation Standards Handbook*. Charlottesville, Virginia: AIMR, 5.

Associated Press (1998). IBM Execs Sought for Questioning, *AP Newswire*, (June 2).

Bok, D. (1976). Can Ethics Be Taught?, *Change* (October), 26-30.

Browne, John (1998). Corporate Responsibility in an International Context, *Ethics in Economics* Nos. 1&2.

Carroll, Archie (1996). *Business & Society: Ethics and Stakeholder Management*, 3rd edition, Cincinnati, OH: Southwestern.

Cohen, J.R., Pant, L.W., and Sharp, D.J. (1993). Culture-Based Ethical Conflicts Confronting Multinational Accounting Firms, *Accounting Horizons* (September), 7 (3), 1-13.

Collins, D. & Wartick, S.L. (1995). Business and Society/Business Ethics Courses, *Business & Society*, Vol. 34, No. 1, 51-89.

Cowton, C.J. and Dunfee, T. (1995). Internationalizing the Business Ethics Curriculum: A Survey, *Journal of Business Ethics* (May), 14, 331-338.

Ferrell, O.C. and Gresham, L.G. (1985). A Contingency Framework for Understanding Ethical Decision Making in Marketing, *Journal of Marketing* (Summer), 49, 87-96.

Ferrell, O.C. and Fraedrich, J. (1997). *Business Ethics: Ethical Decision Making and Cases* (3rd edition) Boston, MA: Houghton-Mifflin.

Fritzsche, David J. (1985). Ethical Issues in Multinational Marketing, *in Marketing Ethics: Guidelines for Managers* by G. Laczniak and Patrick E. Murphy, Lexington, MA: Lexington Books.

Gabbott, Mark (1994). The European Community Framework for Distance Selling, *Journal of Public Policy and Marketing*, 13 (Fall), 307-312.

Glass, Richard S. and Bonnici, Joseph (1997). An Experiential Approach for Teaching Business Ethics, *Teaching Business Ethics*, 1 (2), 183-195.

Goolsby, Jerry R. and Hunt, S.D. (1992). Cognitive Moral Development and Marketing, *Journal of Marketing*, 56 (January), 55-68.

Gordon, R.J. (1993). Why the Principles Course Needs Comparative Macro and Micro. *American Economic Review*, 83(2), 17-22.

Hamid, S., Craig, R., and Clarke, F. (1993). Religion: A Confounding Cultural Element in the International Harmonization of Accounting. *Abacus* 29 (2), 131-148.

Haskins, M.E., Ferris, K.R., and Selling, T.I. (1996). *International Financial Reporting and Analysis: A Contextual Emphasis*, New York: Richard D. Irwin.

Hausman, D. & McPherson, M. (1993). Taking Ethics Seriously: Economics and Contemporary Moral Philosophy, *Journal of Economic Literature*, 31, 671-731.

Hofstede, G. (1980). *Culture's Consequences: International Differences in Work-Related Values*. Beverly Hills, CA: Sage Publications.

Hofstede, G. and Bond, M. (1984). Hofstede's Curltural Dimensions: An Independent Validation Using Rokeach's Value Survey. *Journal of Cross-Cultural Psychology* (December), 15 (4), 417-433.

Hunt, S.D. and Vitell, S. (1986). A General Theory of Marketing Ethics, *Journal of Macromarketing* (Spring), 6, 5-16.

Johnson, D.M. (1992). Professionalism in the Third World. *Internal Auditor* (October), (5), 51-54.

Jones, Ceri (1998). News: Insider dealing–Huge fines for cheats. *Financial Times Business Reports Investors Chronicle*, (May 8) (124), No. 1577, 12.

Jones, Thomas M. (1991). Ethical Decision Making by Individuals in Organizations: An Issue–Contingent Model, *Academy of Management Review* 16 (2), 366–395.

Kalthenhauser, Skip (1998). Bribery is Being Outlawed Worldwide, *Business Ethics*, (May/June), 11.

Kish, Matthew L. (1998). Human Rights & Business: Profiting from Observing Human Rights, *Ethics in Economics*, Nos. 1 & 2, 13.

Mankiw, N.G. (1998). *Principles of Macroeconomics*, Fort Worth: The Dryden Press.

Mankower, Joel (1994), *Beyond the Bottom Line*. Washington, DC: Business for Social Responsibility.

Matlack, Carol (1998). Where Importers Live a Nightmare . . . and Locals Choke on Corruption, *Business Week Online (International Edition)*, May 18.

Murphy, Patrick E. and Laczniak, Gene R. (1981). Marketing Ethics: A Review with Implications for Managers, Educators and Researchers, in *Review of Marketing*, Ben M. Enis and Kenneth J. Roering, eds. Chicago: American Marketing Association, 251-266.

Pizzolatto, A.B. & Bevill, S. (1996). Business Ethics: A Classroom Priority, *Journal of Business Ethics*, 15, 153-158.

Shannon, J. Richare and Berl, Robert L. (1997). Are We Teaching Ethics in Marketing? A Survey of Students' Attitudes and Perceptions, *Journal of Business Ethics*, 16 (July), 1059-1075.

Shari, Michael and Einhorn, Bruce (1998). Indonesia: Graft Won't Just Vanish, *Business Week Online (International Edition)*, June 1.

Stiglitz, J.E. (1993). International Perspectives in Undergraduate Education. *American Economic Review*, 83(2), 27-33.

Thorne LeClair, Debbie, Ferrell, OC and Ferrell, Linda (1997). Federal Sentencing Guidelines for Organizations: Legal, Ethical, and Public Policy Issues for International Marketing, *Journal of Public Policy and Marketing*, 16 (Spring), 26-37.

Transparency International (1998), *1998 Corruption Perception Index*, http://www.transparency.de.

Vega, Gina (1997). Caveat Emptor: Ethical Chauvinism in the Global Economy, *Journal of Business Ethics*, 16 (September), 1353-1362.

Wanner, Barbara (1998). Financial Scandals Renew Focus on Bureaucratic Power (Part 1), *IAC Newsletter Database, Japan Economic Institute of America JEI Report*, (March 6), 9.

Winkle, G.M., Huss, H.F. and Xi-Zhu, C. (1994). Accounting Standards in the People's Republic of China: Responding to Economic Reforms, *Accounting Horizons*, 8 (3), September, 48-57.

Zarzeski, M.T. (1996a). Cultural Clash, *Accountancy-International Edition*, (March), 70-71.

Zarzeski, M.T. (1996b). Spontaneous Harmonization Effects of Cultural and Market Forces on Accounting Disclosure Practices, *Accounting Horizons*, 10 (1), March, 18-37.

Social Responsibility and *Mana* in International Business Education

John Patterson
Glenys Patterson

SUMMARY. Exposure to indigenous philosophies and values such as those of the Maori of New Zealand can contribute to the education of International Business graduates. The Maori link social responsibility with *mana*: those who claim *mana* or standing must practice associated social responsibilities while those who want more *mana* can gain it by taking on new responsibilities. These interrelated connections are described in some detail and applied to International Business. *[Article copies available for a fee from The Haworth Document Delivery Service: 1-800-342-9678. E-mail address: getinfo@haworthpressinc.com <Website: http://www.haworthpressinc.com>]*

KEYWORDS. Social responsibility, international business education, Mana, Maori culture

INTRODUCTION

International Business graduates may be lucky enough to find that the values and world view of their home country are shared throughout the world in which they work. But that is unlikely; even within the

---

John Patterson is with the School of History, Philosophy and Politics, (E-mail: patto@massey.ac.nz) and Glenys Patterson is with the Department of Management Systems at Massey University, Palmerston North, New Zealand.

[Haworth co-indexing entry note]: "Social Responsibility and *Mana* in International Business Education." Patterson, John and Glenys Patterson. Co-published simultaneously in *Journal of Teaching in International Business* (International Business Press, an imprint of The Haworth Press, Inc.) Vol. 11, No. 1, 1999, pp. 73-89; and: *Teaching International Business: Ethics and Corporate Social Responsibility* (ed: Gopalkrishnan R. Iyer) International Business Press, an imprint of The Haworth Press, Inc., 1999, pp. 73-89. Single or multiple copies of this article are available for a fee from The Haworth Document Delivery Service [1-800-342-9678, 9:00 a.m. - 5:00 p.m. (EST). E-mail address: getinfo@haworthpressinc.com].

confines of a single nation it is common enough to find philosophical differences which have significant impacts on business practice and business ethics, and as the scope of a business operation widens from a national arena to an international or multinational one the probability of such differences can be expected to multiply. In a perfect world an International Business graduate would emerge equipped to cope with these differences, being well steeped in the various philosophies involved and skilled in procedures for mediating disagreements. In the real world though this is unlikely to be possible. There are simply too many ways of viewing and valuing the world to master in an entire lifetime, let alone in the few years available for formal education.

So how can we design a curriculum in International Business that will prepare graduates for the diversity of values they are likely to encounter? The solution suggested here is to give a thorough grounding in the philosophy and ethics of a single indigenous or other "alien" society, perhaps not even one the graduates are likely in practice to encounter. The idea is that people who have *mana*ged to take seriously the world view and values of one society that is radically different from their own should be equipped to see the world through the eyes of others, to perceive the presuppositions of their own world view, and thus be less likely to commit ethical or philosophical blunders that may harm their business enterprises or the foreign worlds in which they can expect to have to work.

The aim of this paper is not to provide empirical evidence that such a programme of study is likely to have the desired effect. For such evidence to exist we would have to implement a programme of study of an indigenous society, under scientifically valid control conditions. It would be unwise even to contemplate this without a good idea of just what sort of content could enter into the programme of study. While we certainly must avoid designing a curriculum on the basis of hunches or currently fashionable ideas alone, we also need to be clear about what sort of "alternative" values and philosophies there are "out there," whether they do indeed differ significantly from more familiar western ideas and whether they are interestingly relevant to International Business. So in this exploratory paper what we shall do is simply present some key aspects of one particular indigenous society which we believe are importantly different to their parallels in the conventional International Business curriculum and are in their own

right of considerable interest in business ethics and business philosophy generally.

The philosophy and values concerned are those of the Maori of
New Zealand. The main link with the conventional International Business curriculum is through the familiar idea of Social Responsibility,
the obligation of individuals and organizations to act in ways that
contribute to the interests of society, not only to their own interests.
The distinctively Maori contribution to this topic will make use of the
key concept of *mana*. Briefly, there is a two-way relationship between
responsibility and *mana*: each in a sense entails the other. If a business
or a business person is to gain and maintain the *mana* or standing
needed to operate effectively and with authority they have to accept
the responsibilities that go with that *mana*. On the other hand, one
effective way of gaining *mana* in the first place is to take responsibility for matters which are not strictly speaking your business.

THE NATURE OF MANA

There are important preliminaries to all of this. Apart from having a
good idea of what *mana* is, we need to know about two contrasting
and complementary ways in which it can be gained. For an initial
"definition" of *mana* we can start with the dictionaries, which typically say that *mana* is authority, power, influence, prestige (Metge 1995:
87-90). All these can be of vital importance in international business.
The *mana* or standing of a business will relate to its chances of success. To do well a business must have authority to conduct its operations and the power to make use of that authority. One of the great
strengths of the concept of *mana* is that it brings these two together:
without authority no amount of power can amount to *mana*, but authority without power is not *mana* either. This applies as much to a
business context as to a traditional Maori tribal context.

But these ideas of power and authority are no more than a start to
understanding *mana*. The analysis of *mana* which follows downplays
any "magical" aspect. Granted, in a traditional Maori setting great
mana is frequently associated with practices that might be described as
magical, as for example when the hero Maui uses magical incantations
to fish the North Island of New Zealand up from the bottom of the sea,
both employing and gaining *mana* in the process (Grey 1956: 31-32).
But the association relates more to the beliefs about how states of

affairs are brought about which happen to be current in the community concerned than with any deep element of meaning of *mana*. In different societies *mana* is associated with a wide range of forms of power and authority and can be gained and lost in a range of familiar and straightforward ways. These include the spectacular way of warfare, where great warriors earn fame and power for themselves and their kin through successes in battle, whether nor not magic is believed to play a part in martial success. But they include also the more modest way of generosity, cooperation, and taking responsibility, where any of us can enhance the *mana* of others as well as gain it for ourselves.

There is a tendency in contemporary western philosophy to make a sharp distinction between the descriptive and the evaluative, and while it certainly has its place in philosophical analysis, when approaching concepts from another culture we have to realize that they may incorporate both descriptive and evaluative elements in key philosophical concepts. Indeed we have to be aware of this in the case of many English concepts too: for example the concept of *murder* contains both descriptive and evaluative elements (Kovesi 1967: 26-27, 149-150). *Mana* is like this. Commonly translated as both "power" (descriptive) and "authority" (evaluative), *mana* has to involve both power and authority.

Seeing this interplay of fact and value helps us understand the concept of *mana* in Maori traditions. Time and again an ancestral act is recorded (apparently with approval) which involves great deceit or worse, as for example when Hinauri, sister of the hero Maui, kills her new husband's old wives in order to reveal the precious jade or greenstone hidden in their bodies (Alpers 1964: 75). To understand such incidents and their place in Maori thought, the Maori anthropologist Ranginui Walker tells us we have to understand that the *mana* obtained is valued as a great good, so that the apparently outrageous means are seen as thereby justified (Walker 1978: 22). We should also realize that the *mana* gained in such actions is not only individual *mana*. The *mana* associated with the precious greenstone is the *mana* of a wide community. To kill as Hinauri did for personal gain might not be acceptable; it is the communal *mana* that results which justifies her action. Maintaining tribal *mana* can seem to be the crown of all the Maori virtues (Perrett and Patterson 1991: 193).

In explaining the concept of *mana* some authors such as Maori Marsden (1977: 145) and Cleve Barlow (1991: 61) insist that it is a spiritual authority bestowed by the gods. Others see *mana* primarily in terms of power rather than authority, for example Peter Buck (1950: 353) and Ross Bowden (1979), who wants to distinguish between *mana* as power in comparison with *tapu* as spiritual authority. Given these differences it is probably best to go along with the dictionaries and to follow the example of Joan Metge, who accepts that the concept involves both power and authority (1976: 63-4). In doing this, those who do not want to accept in any literal sense the involvement of spirits in *mana* do not have to do away with the spiritual aspect of the concept. For one thing, even if in traditional Maori context *mana* is seen as coming from the gods, it does not follow that this is a part of the meaning of the concept. A culture which does not share such spiritual beliefs might still have a concept of *mana*. However important it may seem to the insider, a more analytical approach might persuade us that the involvement of gods or spirits is inessential to the concept of *mana* itself.

Often enough it is possible to give an analysis of the spiritual aspect of *mana* in terms of ethical ideas rather than metaphysical ones, interpreting statements that involve the word *mana* not as literal descriptions of a mysterious spiritual world but as straightforward value judgements about the familiar world (Patterson 1992: ch. 2). So for example, if arrogant visitors to a tribe's *marae* or meeting house are accused of trampling on the *mana* of their hosts, they should look to their manners, not to some mysterious force permeating the atmosphere or soil of the *marae*. None of this requires us to deny that there are any spiritual forces, but only that in using the concept of *mana*, even in many of its spiritual aspects, we are not committed thereby to any unfamiliar metaphysics.

COLLECTIVE MANA AND INDIVIDUAL MANA

The story of the discovery of greenstone illustrates how an action which generates *mana* can take on a new perspective when the *mana* involved is seen as collective, not only individual. What would be unacceptable when the end is individual *mana* becomes acceptable and even laudable when tribal *mana* is at stake. In Maori terms, to have *mana* or standing we cannot stand alone; *mana* is essentially as much a collective matter as an individual one. Although traditionally tribal *mana* was and often enough still is focussed at the top of a hierarchical social structure, the *mana* of those in high places was and is also the *mana* of all, even of each individual. Leaders maintain their *mana* and that of their people by attending to the standing of the people collectively.

So, just as the concept of *mana* represents some inseparable intertwining of power and authority, it also represents an inseparable intertwining of individual and collective. In understanding Maori *mana* it is a mistake to think that collective *mana* is simply the sum of the *mana* of the individuals who comprise the collective. Perhaps to counteract this idea, Maori sometimes express the opposite idea, that the communities to which we belong make us who we are, as individual persons (Johansen 1954: 55-56). Between these extremes we can find at least an idealized mean, by letting go of the idea that the individual and the community are really distinct, that either can be adequately accounted for in terms of the other. Instead, see them as so intimately interrelated that there is no way that one of them could be eclipsed by the other. According to this picture, the *mana* of an individual really is the *mana* of that individual, even if it is also an aspect of a tribe's *mana*.

This idealized relationship is expressed by Prytz Johansen in terms of the idea of "kinship life," which he sees as the *mana* of the ancestors flowing down from generation to generation (1954: 149-52). Like inherited wealth, and even perhaps entailed wealth, the fact that it comes from parents and passes on to children does not make it any less one's own. And the connections are also as it were horizontal as well as vertical. The web of kinship extends into the past and into the future, but it also extends widely amongst living kin. Understanding Maori *mana* involves an appreciation of the importance of these webs of kinship, and it might not be too fanciful to describe them as the reinforcing that holds the whole world together not–only the human world but also the ecosystem to which we all belong. Johansen emphasizes this collective aspect when he says that *mana* is an "active fellowship" which is "never inextricably bound up with any single thing or any single human being" (1954: 85).

So even when *mana* is overtly associated with an individual such as a tribal leader, to understand it at all well we need to find out about a whole web of relationships (which are conventionally represented as kinship relationships amongst traditional Maori). And if we see *mana* in this way as essentially relational, we are not so easily puzzled when we ask just what *mana* is. Often when we ask what something is we hope to have some sort of *thing* pointed out to us. If we approach the concept of *mana* with this hope, we run the risk of inventing a rather odd sort of "thing"–perhaps a spiritual substance or force, emanating from a spiritual being. If we want to avoid this sort of impenetrable mystery, we can simply abandon the idea that *mana* is a thing at all, looking instead for relations between perfectly familiar things such as people, tribes and lands. And under this sort of conception of *mana* other mysteries can vanish. If *mana* is a substance, it is rather a mystery how it can come into existence or disappear, but if it is relational there is no problem, as relationships between familiar things can come into and out of existence in ways that are familiar to all of us.

We are wise then at least to leave open the possibility that *mana* consists in certain relations, typically between people and communities of people. This is what is behind Johansen's analysis in terms of "fellowship" and "kinship life." There is one small trap though to beware: in analyzing *mana* in terms of fellowship we must not think only of friendly relationships between people as being involved. These may well be paramount, as is suggested by the fact that the term *manaaki,* meaning literally to make *mana,* is a term commonly used to denote showing respect or kindness to others (Patterson 1994). But for all this it is frequently the case that the *mana* of an individual or community can depend on its hostile relations with others as well as on the friendly ones.

TWO WAYS OF GAINING MANA

From the perspective of International Business, perhaps the most important thing to know about *mana* is how it can be gained (and lost). Start by distinguishing what might be called ascribed *mana* and achieved *mana.* In a traditional Maori culture, each person has a certain degree of *mana* in virtue of "who" that person is seen as being, socially. This ascribed *mana* is or was typically associated with birth, flowing down from ancestors and often favouring the first-born and the male descendants (Ngata in Ngata and Buck 1986: 247), with the amount of *mana* available as it were for distribution depending upon the *mana* of the particular ancestors from whom it flows. This means that those of junior status start out in life at a disadvantage. But the disadvantage is not necessarily permanent. Those of junior status can gain great *mana* through their deeds (Pere 1982: 32). Probably the best-known traditional examples involve the folk-hero Maui, one of whose names, Maui-potiki, records his junior ranking, *potiki* meaning youngest child. Despite this initial disadvantage, Maui achieved enormous *mana* through his prodigious deeds. We have met his discovery of the precious greenstone; he is also remembered for slowing down the sun in its journey across the sky, gaining the secret of fire from his ancestress, catching the fish which is now known as the North Island of New Zealand, and very nearly overcoming death itself (Alpers 1964: 28-70).

As far as achieved *mana* is concerned, there are two crucially different paths to *mana*, which we might call the path of *hard mana* and the path of *soft mana*. These can be nicely illustrated from within Maori traditional narratives, where for example the god Tane-mahuta, ancestor of trees and of the Maori people, gains great *mana* by tearing asunder his parents Earth and Sky and thus allowing in the light and air needed by their children for proper growth (Grey 1971: 1-2; Grey 1956: 2). This is a fierce aggressive act. This is the way of hard *mana*. But when Tane-mahuta sees the sorry state of his parents he takes pity on them, covering his mother the Earth with protecting forests and decorating his lonely father the Sky with stars. This is an act of compassion. This is the way of soft *mana*. In protecting and decorating his parents Tane restores to them some of the *mana* they have lost, and Tane himself in turn gains *mana* from these kindly deeds. Not only is he remembered in song, story and carving as the separator of Earth and Sky, but he is also familiar as the father of the forests and the decorator of the heavens. He gains *mana* from his aggressive acts (hard *mana*), and he also gains *mana* from his supportive acts (soft *mana*). As is so often the case, in gaining hard *mana* he takes *mana* from others in order to win it for himself, whereas in gaining soft *mana* he adds to the *mana* of others as well as his own. While in the way of hard *mana* there are losers as well as winners, in the way of soft *mana* there can be winners without there being any losers.

Students of International Business might pause here to think of examples of businesses that have achieved hard *mana* and others that have achieved soft *mana*. The former come easily to mind, being in accord with familiar stereotypes of the tough competitive businessman, but the alternative way of soft *mana* also has a place in international business, a place that is gaining increasing recognition. The suggestion of this paper is that it could have a much more important place, that businesses which want to build up their *mana* in an international setting might do well to look to the cooperative, supportive ways of soft *mana* rather than rely solely on the competitive, aggressive ways of hard *mana* which are all too familiar.

MANA AND SOCIAL RESPONSIBILITY

The link with business philosophy can be forged more closely by seeing that the idea of soft *mana* helps to bring to life the two-way link between *mana* and social responsibility. If we are to claim *mana* in a country we have to take some responsibility for its wellbeing, otherwise we stand to lose that *mana*, and taking responsibility involves the sort of caring and cooperation that characterize the way of soft *mana*. On the other hand if we do *mana*ge to take responsibility for or in a country we also stand to gain *mana* there; this is precisely the way of soft *mana*.

Look first at the way in which *mana* entails responsibility. According to this view of our place in the world, all of us are responsible for the areas that come under our *mana*. This applies to geographical areas: for example, a Maori tribe that holds *mana* over an area of land, the *tangata whenua* or people of the land, see themselves and are seen by others as responsible for what goes on within their lands. But this is so not only in geographical areas: people who claim special expertise or authority would be seen as responsible for what goes on within the field concerned. For example the medical profession would be seen as responsible for health, and their *mana* as medical experts and authorities depends upon their ability to see to the health of the people. Precisely the same holds for business enterprises and practitioners. In particular the social underpinning of the authority (*mana*) to conduct business is related to a willingness and ability to take at least some responsibility for the well-being of the society of which a business forms a part.

STRICT RESPONSIBILITY

A fuller idea of the relations between *mana* and social responsibility can be found by studying Maori practices, such as the practice of *muru*, a form of *utu* or reciprocity (Patterson 1992: ch. 5). At least in former times, if someone of great standing suffered a calamity there was a distinct possibility that some of their kin would descend upon them and plunder whatever might be left of their possessions. Such raids are called *muru*, and can appear a great mystery, at least to the outsider (Buck 1950: 421; Johansen 1954: 145; Maning 1930: 98-100). Why do people fall upon their kin in their hour of greatest need? Surely they should on the contrary be supporting one another in times of misfortune? A non-Maori would be outraged at this sort of behaviour. So, what is the explanation? It seems to be something like this: if I suffer great misfortune it shows that I have been unable to exercise my *mana*, I have been unable to exercise my social responsibilities, my world has not been under my control. It is up to me to look after my lands, my property, my dependents. That is my responsibility (Johansen 1954: 142). If it becomes clear that at least for a while these responsibilities are beyond me, someone has to take them over. Someone from the wider kinship group, that is, kinship solidarity being of immense importance in Maori. Hence the *muru* raid, which removes such remaining goods and even dependent people to a safer place, until such time as I show that my *mana* is reestablished, until such time as I show that I am able to take responsibility once more. Rather than being outraged at the *muru* raid I might well be flattered, in that it amounts to a public recognition of the extent of my *mana*. If my wider kin group had not responded in the conventional way it might mean that they did not fully acknowledge my own *mana*.

This shows that the responsibility associated with *mana* can be independent of one's intentions (Maning 1930: 64). This Maori perspective is in striking contrast with a familiar western way of thinking about responsibility, the idea that we are not responsible for anything unless we deliberately bring it about. According to this there are two related conditions necessary for responsibility. The first is a matter of causation; I cannot be held responsible for anything unless I myself bring it about. If I can show that somebody else spilled the wine on the carpet then I have shown that it is not my responsibility. The second condition is a matter of intention; I cannot be held responsible for anything unless I intentionally bring it about. So if I am forced to admit that it was indeed my wine that landed on the carpet, I might still try to evade responsibility by showing that somebody else knocked into me. Both of these are familiar patterns of thinking, even if they may not always be accepted as valid. For example, despite the fact that I was jostled I might be held responsible for the stained carpet on the ground that I should have known that the room was crowded, the carpet was pale, and the wine red. I might from time to time be held responsible even when I play no causal role at all. But on the whole, according to this conception of responsibility, both causation and intention are necessary conditions for responsibility.

One thing that happens if we do regard both intention and causation as necessary for responsibility is that commonly there is nobody at all who can be held "really" responsible when things go wrong. Many of the conditions that emerge from our complex social and economic interactions are not brought about by anybody at all, and certainly not intentionally. For example each and every individual and corporation might try to disclaim responsibility for the sorry state of the natural environment, or of the stock market, on the grounds that we did not intentionally bring it about. Just how plausible the disclaimer might be is another matter, but the point is that, given the way we are used to thinking about responsibility it is easy for us at least to feel that the state of the environment is not our responsibility, because (we feel) we did not bring it about, and certainly not intentionally.

A *mana*-based conception of responsibility can remove this way of opting out. Under a *mana*-based conception, intention is irrelevant to questions of responsibility, and so is causation. If I have *mana* over an area, then I am responsible for whatever goes on in that area, period. I am not responsible in a moral sense, though, and herein lies perhaps another difference between the two conceptions. Under a western as opposed to a Maori conception of responsibility, if I fall down in my responsibilities then I can be held to blame, morally. Although no doubt the same consideration can arise under a *mana*-based conception, considerations of prudence and collective solidarity seem to be more prominent than considerations of morality. If something goes wrong in the sphere of my responsibility the pressing question is, what can I do to restore my *mana*? Even if it were socially acceptable to avail myself of the "excuse" that I was not the actual cause of what went wrong, to do so would be likely to threaten my *mana* even further: not only have I failed to exercise the responsibility entailed by my *mana* but I am as it were denying that I had the responsibility in the first place, which amounts to denying that I had the *mana*. Further, responsibility as conceived by the Maori is also a highly collective matter (Patterson 1992a), so in all of this the "I" can as easily be a corporation as an individual. Under a *mana*-based conception of responsibility a corporation will be most unwise to opt out of social responsibility on the grounds that it did not intentionally bring about some state of affairs. That simply invites others to step in and accept the responsibility, thus standing to gain the associated *mana*, and all of the associated authority and power.

It is not being suggested though that we dismiss intention and causation as irrelevant. All that is being argued is that in some situations a *mana*-based concept can have important applications even outside of a Maori context. One is in the field of leadership, which is always important in business. In a Maori context, leaders have to take responsibility for all manner of things for which they are not causally responsible. Effectively, they live in a world of strict liability (Johansen 1954: 130-134). Leaders who turn out to be unable or unwilling to put matters to rights risk losing their positions as leaders. This is familiar enough in western contexts too. Political leaders for example may be experts at blaming other people for any troubles that pop up when they are not looking, but they should know that they are likely to be held responsible anyway. The same goes for institutional and business leaders. There is a saying, "the buck stops here": it might be possible to shift blame for troubles a certain way but in any situation there tends to be a point at which this is no longer accepted. The Chairman of the Board or the Chief Executive Officer may have had no hand in the troubles an organization is experiencing, but unless they can come up with a solution they are likely to lose some of their authority if not their jobs. If they do not put matters right the *mana* they need to hold onto their positions of leadership can be lost.

We might expand on this in terms of authority. Leaders are typically in positions of some sort of authority. One of the conventional ways of translating *mana* is as "authority," and certainly there can be no authority without *mana*. Thus if *mana* entails responsibility, so too does authority. If those in authority, whether it be "lawful" authority or less formal authority, refuse to accept responsibility for something that goes on within the field of that authority, their *mana* stands to diminish thereby, and hence their authority also stands to diminish. Questions of who is "responsible" in a causal sense are irrelevant to this. A clear example can be found in the case of the police and associated legal authorities. If the police fail to keep crime under control their *mana* suffers, and whatever their formal standing in law may be, their authority amongst the community also suffers. This need have nothing to do with whether they had the resources to control crime. We may be sympathetic to them for being expected to do something that was effectively impossible, but still their *mana* and authority suffer, and will continue to suffer until the police find an effective and acceptable way of regaining control.

These examples show that although Maori provide the obvious source of a *mana*-based conception of responsibility, it is already a familiar conception, if not as familiar as it needs to be. A causal conception of responsibility is perhaps understandable when responsibility is thought of as mostly an individual matter. It certainly can be used to help preserve individual rights. Few of us could hope as individuals to exercise any significant control over any significant area of the globe, and for that reason no doubt we might find a non-causal idea of responsibility an intolerable burden. But if responsibility is thought of in a more collective manner, as is appropriate in a business setting, a *mana*-based concept is more attractive, at least insofar as a community or corporation or organization could be expected to have a better chance of exercising effective control over a significant area than could an individual.

GAINING MANA BY TAKING RESPONSIBILITY

Look now at the other side of the link between responsibility and *mana*. Not only does *mana* entail responsibility, but the link goes in the opposite direction as well. If we *mana*ge to *take* responsibility for something we stand to *gain mana* thereby. A clear example is found in the traditional narrative relating the disputes between the children of Earth and Sky, where some of the children of Tangaroa the sea-god take refuge in the forests of Tane-mahuta. Tane takes it upon himself to look after them, and thereby gains *mana* over them at the expense of their natural parent, his brother Tangaroa (Grey 1971: 2-3; Grey 1956: 5-6). The question does not arise whether these refugees had any *right* to Tane's hospitality. The question is resolved in terms of *mana*: the forests are under the *mana* of Tane, he being the godly ancestor who made them in order to clothe his mother, the Earth, after he separated her from his father, the Sky. His *mana* over the forests gives him two options: he can either follow the way of hard *mana*, exercising his *mana* aggressively by repelling the intruders, or he can follow the way of soft *mana*, caring for them as he does the other creatures in his forests.

To enhance our understanding of the way that *mana* can be generated or earned through taking responsibility, we might call upon the idea that nature hates a vacuum. If there is a place in the business or natural or social world in which nobody has effective *mana* then there is an opportunity for some enterprising creature or corporation to step in. Sometimes this might be done aggressively, as when a vigorous species rapidly establishes itself almost exclusively in an area after some ecological breakdown, quickly laying claim to a territory and vigorously excluding a range of other species, or when an sharp-witted or lucky entrepreneur makes a sudden killing. But as the story about Tane and Tangaroa illustrates, it can also be done in a non-competitive way, achieving soft *mana* rather than hard *mana*, as no doubt was often the case when mutually interdependent species slowly evolved together, the biological standing of each species coming to depend upon that of an increasing range of other species, until a stable complex ecosystem emerged. Now it is not suggested that these examples from ecology are literally cases of taking responsibility, but for all that they are a useful model for us when we are looking at ways we might come to fit better into the world in which we live. Seizing upon opportunities for cooperation can be just as effective for establishing our *mana* as are the more spectacular cases of seizing upon opportunities for competition (Odum 1992). In a way cooperation is a better bet insofar as competition tends to generate losers as well as winners while well-judged cooperation can generate winners all round. Unless we can be fairly sure of ending up as the winners rather than the losers, we are well advised to opt for the way of soft *mana*.

EARNING MANA THROUGH SOCIAL RESPONSIBILITY IN BUSINESS

In a business context the point of developing this idea of earning *mana* through taking environmental responsibility should be fairly clear. Although individuals or companies may with some justification disclaim responsibility for the economic and ecological state of the planet, it is still open to anybody to *take* a degree of responsibility. Even though as individuals or companies we may succeed on only a tiny scale, at least on that scale we do stand to earn *mana*, to earn for ourselves a place to stand, whether this be an ecological niche or a business one. Collectively we can do much more, both in terms of creating win-win situations in the natural environment and in terms of creating win-win situations in the world of business.

Remember here the crucial aspect of the way of soft *mana*-that both sides stand to gain. If we do *mana*ge to extend the sphere of our responsibility, especially if we take collective responsibility, the world in which we live and work stands to gain just as much as we do if not more. The details of how we might take this responsibility will no doubt vary from place to place and from time to time, but there are some principles that might constitute a good beginning for any of us. If we are to change from being exploiters of one another and of the planet to being responsible care-takers, a first move is to reflect on how we conceive of ourselves in relation to others. Do we see ourselves as the centre of the universe? Not a good beginning for a business philosophy which hopes to highlight the path of soft *mana*. If we hope to follow the path of soft *mana* in earning our place in the international communities in which we live we need to accept that others too have *mana*, that our *mana* does not exclude theirs. If we are to accept the responsibilities that spring from whatever *mana* we hold we have to see the others that contribute to that *mana* as standing alongside us, not *under* us. In terminology familiar in business literature, we must acknowledge their standing as stakeholders: to acknowledge a party as a stakeholder simply is to acknowledge its standing or *mana* in the community concerned. To have *mana* simply is to have a stake.

This means that the all too familiar idea that the only way to go about business is the way of the corporate warrior needs to be abandoned. Although this might sound odd in relation to a people noted for its warriors, if we are genuinely to accept in practice that others have *mana* in the areas where we operate, we might start by acknowledging in a practical way that our own *mana* does not exclude that of others and indeed requires it. That applies as much to the warriors of a tribal society as to anybody else. By acknowledging the interdependence of the *mana* of all parties to a business relation, we can come to forge cooperative bonds with all who share the world in which we do business, as parts of a larger whole. We do not need to place ourselves below them, of course, and neither do we need to place the whole above the parts. But we cannot expect to get far in practice along the path to soft *mana* in international business if we see ourselves as somehow superior to others. We may be bigger, in economic terms, but that may not mean that we have any great standing in anything but the business community. To have the standing we need in local communities we are wise to become in a real sense working parts of those communities, not outsiders who merely use them for our own ends.

Finally, how might these ideas be incorporated into a curriculum? No doubt there is a variety of ways that students of International Business might gain a deep understanding of the places where they are to work, one obvious way being long and rich experience gained working within the societies concerned. Short of that, though, the curriculum might at least provide some basic insights and sensitivities. A thorough grounding in the values and world view of at least one indigenous society can make an important contribution. This can be expected to make students more aware of the fact that different societies do have significantly different philosophies, philosophies which have a very real impact on the way business needs to be conducted in a country. For example any business which tried to operate in New Zealand without acknowledging the deeply communal aspects of Maori philosophy could expect to run into real trouble sooner or later. That is as it were the defensive side of the story: if we do not equip ourselves to find out about differences in values and philosophy from place to place our business activities may suffer. But there is also a positive side, well illustrated by the analysis of *mana* presented here. By taking aboard some elements of Maori philosophy and learning to follow the way of soft *mana* any business anywhere in the world can hope to bring rewards not only to itself but also to those with whom it interacts. This message is not particularly easy to state in terms of the concepts which loom large in the business curriculum. In this respect a study of the philosophy and ethics of the Maori of New Zealand can be a rewarding element of a curriculum aimed at preparing International Business graduates for the diversity of values they can expect to encounter in their working careers.

REFERENCES

Alpers, Antony (1964). *Maori Myths and Tribal Legends.* Auckland: Longman Paul.

Barlow, Cleve (1991). *Tikanga Whakaaro: Key Concepts of Maori Culture.* Auckland: Oxford University Press.

Bowden, Ross (1979). Tapu and *Mana*: Ritual Authority and Political Power in Traditional Maori Society. *Journal of Pacific History* 14, 50-61.

Buck, Sir Peter (1950). *The Coming of the Maori*. Second Edition. Wellington: Maori Purposes Fund Board.

Grey, Sir George (1956). *Polynesian Mythology*. Illustrated New Zealand Edition. Christchurch: Whitcombe and Tombs.

Grey, Sir George (1971). *Nga Mahi A Nga Tupuna*. 4th edition. Wellington: A.H. & A.W. Reed.

Johansen, J. Prytz (1954). *The Maori and his Religion in its Non-ritualistic Aspects*. Copenhagen: Munksgaard.

Kovesi, Julius (1967). *Moral Notions*. London: Routledge and Kegan Paul.

Maning, F.E. (1930). *Old New Zealand*. Christchurch: Whitcombe and Tombs.

Marsden, Maori (1977). God, Man and Universe: A Maori View. Michael King (ed), *Te Ao Hurihuri: The World Moves On*. Wellington: Hicks Smith, revised edition.

Metge, Dame Joan (1976). *The Maoris of New Zealand: Rautahi*. Revised edition. London: Routledge and Kegan Paul.

Metge, Dame Joan (1995). *New Growth from Old: The Whanau in the Modern World*. Wellington: Victoria University Press.

Ngata, Sir Apirana, and Sir Peter Buck (1986). *Na To Hoa Aroha: From Your Dear Friend*. Correspondence 1925-50, edited by M.P.K. Sorrenson. Auckland: Auckland University Press. Volume 1.

Odum, Eugene (1992). Great Ideas in Ecology for the 1990s. *BioScience* 42, 542-5.

Patterson, John (1992). *Exploring Maori Values*. Palmerston North: Dunmore Press.

Patterson, John (1992a). A Maori Concept of Collective Responsibility. G. Oddie and R. Perrett (eds.) *Justice, Ethics and New Zealand Society*. Auckland: Oxford University Press.

Patterson, John (1994). Maori Environmental Virtues. *Environmental Ethics* 16, 397-409.

Pere, Rangimarie Rose (1982). *Ako: Concepts and Learning in the Maori Tradition*. Hamilton: University of Waikato, Department of Sociology.

Perrett, Roy, and John Patterson (1991). Virtue Ethics and Maori Ethics. *Philosophy East and West* 41, 185-202.

Walker, Ranginui (1978). The Relevance of Maori Myths and Tradition. Michael King (ed), *Tihe Mauri Ora: Aspects of Maoritanga* Wellington: Methuen, 19-32.

International Corporate Responsibility and MBA Programs: Using an Integrated Approach

Irene M. Herremans
Ron Murch

SUMMARY. This paper discusses an experiential learning situation that can successfully integrate corporate values and international growth in MBA programs. The objective is to present students with a values-led, entrepreneurial focus through "real world" experiences in an integrated context. The article discusses a teaching technique that emphasizes the realistic challenges that corporations face when growing an international company that is built on a strong ethical foundation. *[Article copies available for a fee from The Haworth Document Delivery Service: 1-800-342-9678. E-mail address: getinfo@haworthpressinc.com <Website: http://www.haworthpressinc.com>]*

KEYWORDS. Corporate responsibility, MBA, experiential education, international expansion, values-led

Lead with Your Values and Make Money, Too

–Ben Cohen and Jerry Greenfield

INTRODUCTION

This paper discusses a teaching technique that uses an experiential learning situation to help students understand corporate responsibility

---

Irene M. Herremans and Ron Murch are affiliated with the University of Calgary-Management, 2500 University Dr. NW, Calgary, Alberta, Canada T2N 1N4 (E-mail: herremans@mgmt.ucalgary.ca, or murch@mgmt.ucalgary.ca).

[Haworth co-indexing entry note]: "International Corporate Responsibility and MBA Programs: Using An Integrated Approach." Herremans, Irene M., and Ron Murch. Co-published simultaneously in *Journal of Teaching in International Business* (International Business Press, an imprint of The Haworth Press, Inc.) Vol. 11, No. 1, 1999, pp. 91-117; and: *Teaching International Business: Ethics and Corporate Social Responsibility* (ed: Gopalkrishnan R. Iyer) International Business Press, an imprint of The Haworth Press, Inc., 1999, pp. 91-117. Single or multiple copies of this article are available for a fee from The Haworth Document Delivery Service [1-800-342-9678, 9:00 a.m. - 5:00 p.m. (EST). E-mail address: getinfo@haworthpressinc.com].

91

in an international setting. Although at this time, there is limited evidence to suggest that the technique would be useful in MBA programs in general, it has been applied successfully (based on both faculty and student feedback) in two MBA university programs in different countries, Canada and England. At each university, the process was adapted to meet the particular needs of the program. However, the basic conceptual framework was instrumental in accomplishing two broad-based learning objectives:

- understanding corporate responsibility or values-led strategy in an international business setting.
- integration of traditional functional disciplines (such as accounting, human resources, strategy, information systems, etc.).

This paper discusses the framework used to convey the learning concepts embedded in corporate ethics in any business setting; corporate ethics in an international business setting; and corporate sustainability as it influences decisions of strategy, marketing, accounting, information systems, human resource management, and other traditional business disciplines. Some broad general guidelines are also presented to aid its adaptation to a variety of other settings. Certain variables within the process can easily be changed to accommodate differences in program characteristics and still accomplish the mission of studying a values-led strategy in an international business setting using an integrative approach.

CORPORATE ETHICS–IS IT IMPORTANT?

Corporate ethics drives value-based decisions. Intuitively, one would like to believe that an organization that is perceived to be consistent in applying its values would tend to sustain its business presence for a longer time than others who might not. Even though there is no strong evidence that supports this suggestion, several studies do link favorable corporate responsibility reputations with both stronger financial performance (for example, see Wokutch & Spencer, 1987; Sturdivant et al., 1985; Cochran & Wood, 1984) and less risk (Herremans et al., 1993); consequently, these studies would suggest that more responsible corporations would be more sustainable. More recently, books such as *Built to Last* (Collins and Porras, 1998) and

The Living Company (De Geus, 1997), have emphasized that sustainability applies to more than just the green environment and our natural resources. It has become a decidedly central issue in the decisions that executives make in the conduct of their businesses.

Often, when discussing an organization's ability to manage ethical behavior, we think in terms of the *formal* systems of rules, regulations, and policies (the formal system) that should be in place to prevent any breaches. However, the *informal* systems of shared values, the open lines of communication, and the role models (the informal system) are frequently more important in preventing such abuses (Falkenberg & Herremans, 1995). Noreen (1988) suggests that "certain kinds of ethical behavior lubricate social and economic systems," thus reducing the costs of maintaining a formal prevention system. Furthermore, White (1980) warns that, to the extent that corporations believe that formality alone will generate ethical behavior, they are likely to ignore the real causes of many of the most serious infractions and fail to correct the situation.

In a recent risk management survey conducted by Coopers & Lybrand, personnel issues, inadequate communication, and complacency were cited as reasons for control failures (Update, 1998, p. 14). Often, these "people aspects" are not given adequate attention when managing risk. Even investors, in the process of making investment decisions, often look at intangible aspects before using the hard facts. Serious investors are beginning to consider the reputation of a company to be the most important criterion for investment decision-making–out-ranking both stock performance and financial strength of the company (SRI International as reported by Scott & Smith, 1992, p. 5). Shareholder disapproval, especially when channelled through strong institutional investors, can effectively change the direction of a company's activities. Angel and Rivoli (1997) have shown that large, fast-growing, riskier firms can experience an increase in their costs of capital when they are actively avoided by a large portion of investors–especially in the development of ethical funds portfolios.

INTERNATIONAL BUSINESS MEANS DIFFERENT VALUES

Recent increases in international activities due to multi-lateral international trade agreements, international alliances, and other forms of cooperative agreements have meant that organizations from a number of differing cultures are "bumping shoulders" more frequently. This often results in disagreements over ethical philosophies and differing interpretations of those philosophies. It is essential that our future organizational leaders have a strong sense of their own core values before attempting to sort out complex, international ethical issues in which those core values might clash.

Even though the concept of an international, corporate code of ethics has existed for some time, most early codes have focused on the relationship of the multinational corporation (MNC) with host governments, the general public, and individual persons. There has been an explicit attempt to "lessen the conflict" the corporation might otherwise encounter in fulfilling its primarily economic objectives.

More recently, a new international code of ethics, called the Caux Round Table Principles for Business, has been developed by influential supporters from Europe, Japan, and the United States. The seven Caux Principles are built on two basic ethical ideals:

> *kyosei*-living and working together for the common good enabling co-operation and mutual prosperity to coexist with healthy and fair competition.

> *human dignity*-the value of each person as an end, not simply as a means, to the fulfillment of others' purposes. (The Caux Round Table Principles for Business, 1994)

The Caux Principles represent a long-term, sustainable approach to the role that corporations play in society and suggest that there should be a more deliberate balance among the social, economic, and ecological dimensions of a corporation's activities. They support a more holistic approach to ethical behaviour rather than lists of "thou shall" or "thou shall not." Corporate sustainability has been discussed extensively in the context of environmental stewardship and can be depicted as having three dimensions: economic, social, and ecological/environmental (see Figure1).

Three of the seven Caux Principles show a strong similarity to these dimensions in that they address similar values:

- the responsibilities of an organization beyond the shareholders;
- the economic and social impact of business;
- respect for the environment.

FIGURE 1. The Sustainability Triad

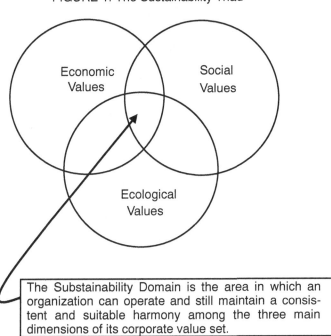

Economic
Values

Social
Values

Ecological
Values

The Substainability Domain is the area in which an organization can operate and still maintain a consistent and suitable harmony among the three main dimensions of its corporate value set.

Until recently, the sustainability concept has been used primarily in the context of environmental stewardship. It has directed our attention to environmental problems and has placed little emphasis on the social dimension of sustainability. Theoretically, all three dimensions (economic, social, and ecological) must be given harmonized emphasis to achieve true sustainability. In the context of international business operations, firms will only sustain themselves when harmony is deliberately maintained among all three dimensions. Ultimately, the personal values of the owners/managers of the business and society's values will act together to determine the strength of the emphasis on any one of the aspects in this "sustainability triad."

In its own right, the term "sustainability" is an abstract concept that seems simple enough to understand. "Sustainable" means capable of being maintained (*Webster's Unabridged Dictionary*, 1983, p. 1,838). Further clarification comes from its derivative "sustain" which means to "keep in existence; keep going; to carry the weight or burden of; or to bear up against" (*Webster's Unabridged Dictionary,* 1983, p. 1,838). An activity, project, or process is termed sustainable if it maintains, supports, or carries the weight or burden of all three dimensions (economic, social, and ecological) in a harmonized manner in either a domestic or international context. (See Milne, 1996, p. 137 on the origin of the integration of these three dimensions.)

THE IMPERATIVE FOR CHANGE

Many MBA programs have recently assessed the appropriateness of their missions, strategies, and objectives as well as the adequacy and relevancy of their course materials, instructional processes, and evaluation methods. Much of this has been in response to a major criticism from employers that MBA programs lack integration among functional areas. For example, employers have felt that students have not fully appreciated how a breakeven analysis, as studied in accounting courses, applies directly to the marketing analyses necessary for launching a new product. As well, students have not understood how strategic direction, studied in policy courses, should drive the deployment of management information systems and reward systems.

Even more importantly, graduating students without a grounding in ethics have shown little appreciation for why issues of ethical values, corporate responsibility, and sustainability should be considered as integral aspects of every corporate decision (Gautschi & Jones, 1998; Menzel, 1997). At the same time, practising business leaders have been voicing that it is essential that these concepts are studied, understood, and internalized as important elements of all issues that managers face day-in and day-out. They are not aspects that can be dealt with only at times of urgency and crisis (Kuhn, 1998; Lazere, 1997).

As important topics for both MBA and professional development programs, the study of corporate ethics is strongly promoted by professionals in the Canadian and United States' financial communities. In a recent study of Canadian-based, international firms and their need for employees to be versed in international financial and accounting topics, chief financial officers and controllers ranked ethics 9th out of 32 international finance and accounting topics as important for inclusion in MBA curricula (Herremans & Wright, 1992). This view is even stronger among government employees who are engaged in negotiating trade agreements as well as settling trade disputes. In a similar study, Canadian government accountants ranked ethical issues 3rd out of the same 32 topics as important for professional educational programs, and 4th out of 32 topics as important for MBA programs (Herremans & Wright, 1994). Furthermore, in the United States, chief financial officers ranked ethical behavior as the most important personal attribute for a graduate (Lazere, 1997).

MBA programs are beginning to recognize the imperative for effective ways to develop their students with an active appreciation for the integrated complexities of leading an organization through value-based dilemmas and the inherent, ethical challenges presented by international operations. " . . . [T]hese issues of ethics and corporate responsibility are at the centre of corporate leadership and, therefore, must be at the centre of management education" (Piper, 1998).

METHODS OF INTEGRATION–PROGRAM STRUCTURE

The issue of teaching international business topics as a separate course or teaching them as part of an existing course has been debated for many years without a definite solution. The same debate has existed regarding corporate ethics. What works for one program of instruction might not work for another, given different time, financial, and other constraints. Regardless of the method used, there seems to be agreement that better education is provided if students can recognize application of the theories and can apply the concepts themselves in an experiential learning situation (Evans, 1992; Novak, 1984).

One of the more deliberate instructional methods used in a program to bring a broad, integrative focus to a variety of issues is referred to in this paper as an Integrated Business Experience (IBE). Within the IBE, there is generally at least one, but there may be several Integrated Sessions (IS). For this paper, an IS is a focused block of active learning that usually takes place in an extended class period (usually one-half day to one day long) but could be held over several days. The complete set of activities and learning elements that occurs both before and after a specific Integrated Session (IS) and includes the IS itself is defined as the integrated business experience (IBE). The IS provides the experience around which the learning activities are structured. To understand an IBE, it requires one to go outside the traditional context of what instructors may generally refer to as a classroom experience. A full IBE process includes preparation for one or more

ISs, perhaps using a number of non-traditional methods of instruction and learning both in and out of the classroom; then participation in an IS; and finally the follow-up to the IS, again using many non-traditional methods of instruction and learning. During the entire IBE process, students analyze problems in an integrative fashion by identifying fundamental and crucial organizational situations and recommending approaches for addressing them. The relationship between the IBE and the IS is illustrated below.

Integrated Business Experience (IBE)

<u>preparation</u>   /integrated activity (IS)/   follow-up

IBEs are set up so that students can derive learning from an experience. The concept is based on the necessity to provide opportunities for individuals "to get a due sense of their own capacity to learn," (Evans, 1992) especially in the dynamic, evolutionary society of the 21st century that requires life-long learning. Experiential learning makes use of life and work experiences that are generally informally acquired. The instructor uses these experiences to develop a learning situation that combines theory with practice in such a manner that will allow students to realize how much they really know. Evans (1992, p. 41) has stated this process of realization as follows: "Most people know more than they think they know if only they knew that they know it."

IBEs should focus on a complex situation faced by a single organization and have multiple faculty members who lead the sessions to reinforce the integrative emphasis. Although there might be one or two lead faculty, it is even better if as many as five or six professors can be involved with a single IBE session in some way. During these sessions, the emphasis is on the higher learning levels of Bloom's taxonomy, especially analysis, synthesis, decision-making, evaluation, and judgment (Bloom, 1956).

Even though sessions can take on many different themes, the one described in this paper deals with sustaining corporate values in the face of changing ownership and developing an international business profile. The timing of the session is flexible and should consider the particular characteristics and geographic location of the MBA program; however, the session should be planned with consideration of the students' level of academic sophistication. When planning an IBE to develop corporate values in an international setting, the students should have a broad appreciation for the strategic implications of personal and corporate value sets, and they should be able to deal capably with multi-dimensional issues. Addressing the actual practice of the theories of corporate responsibility and ethics seems to work best in an IBE when it is a part of a discussion of other corporate operational issues. Consequently, the content and processes are deliberately designed to deal with more than the ethical nature of the decision.

THE INTEGRATED BUSINESS EXPERIENCE (IBE)

The explanation that follows provides details on a learning experience in the form of an IBE that took place at the University of Calgary in Calgary, Alberta, Canada, and then, about six months later, at the Henley Management College in Henley-on-Thames, Greenlands, Oxfordshire, England. Specific learning objectives, the materials used, and the processes that the students went through are described. Although the same company was used as a focus for the experiential portion of the experience, several changes were made to adapt the experience to each program. A framework is also presented that offers guidelines so that learning activities can occur at other universities that wish to accomplish similar objectives. A variety of learning approaches were combined to make students more aware of an international corporation's stewardship role to society and the actions that must be taken to evidence that stewardship. Most importantly, the experience involved the study and analysis of an actual company. The students were put in the position of wrestling with some of the "real" values-based issues the company was facing in becoming an international operation. The experience also included the actual involvement of representatives from the company in some of the activities.

Choice of Company

The subject company for both the University of Calgary's and the Henley Management College's experience was Ben & Jerry's Homemade, Inc. However, other companies could be used as well. Company characteristics that are helpful in making the experience successful are as follows:

1. Recognition of the company as implementing a values-led strategy.
2. Openness in communicating its values-led strategy through its corporate communications vehicles, such as its annual report, environmental report, social audit, code of ethics or credo, and operations plan.
3. Public availability of the corporate communications vehicles and materials.
4. Some media coverage of the company's values-led strategy, as well as its business strategy, that is available through the public press or periodical databases.
5. Academic or business cases written on the company's values-led strategy, as well as its business strategy.
6. Willingness of the company to participate in the experience in some way.

Ben & Jerry's Homemade, Inc. is a company that meets all of the above criteria and therefore was the choice of company for this experience. However, the activities of similar companies could easily be substituted for this experience. Some potential company candidates might be Starbucks, The Body Shop, Virgin, and Johnson & Johnson.

Ben & Jerry's Homemade, Inc. is named after its founders, Ben Cohen and Jerry Greenfield. They have integrated their personal values and way of life into their business philosophy. In 1978 the company started out as a single ice cream scoop shop with the objective to make enough money to give something back to the community of Burlington in the state of Vermont in the United States (Cohen & Greenfield, 1997). By 1995 (the time setting for the basic business case used in these sessions), the company had grown into a US$160 million international company facing difficult questions about using the business as a tool for social change as it grows internationally. Since its inception, the company has been guided by its three-part social mission:

> Ben & Jerry's is dedicated to the creation and demonstration of a new corporate concept of linked prosperity. Our mission consists of three interrelated parts: Product, Economic and Social.

Product: To make, distribute and sell the finest quality all natural ice cream and related products in a wide variety of innovative flavours made from Vermont dairy products.

Economic: To operate the company on a sound financial basis of profitable growth, increasing value for our shareholders and creating career opportunities and financial rewards for our employees.

Social: To operate the company in a way that actively recognizes the central role that business plays in the structure of society by initiating innovative ways to improve the quality of life of a broad community: local, national and international.

The company operates in the United States, Canada, Israel, and several countries in Europe. It has a vision of continued international growth. However, it recently discontinued its operations in Russia and was forced to face some difficult philosophical issues (involving its operations in France) due to France's policies on nuclear testing. Although not all students will agree with Ben & Jerry's philosophy of corporate responsibility, the company and the situation it was facing in 1995 provides an excellent vehicle for students to think about the compatibility of social, ecological, and economic issues. Key aspects of the company's values-led strategy that were discussed at both Calgary and Henley follow:

- What activities render the three dimensions of their mission compatible?
- What activities render them incompatible?
- Is the "values-led" approach (successful in the United States) appropriate for its international operations?
- Is the company practising cultural imperialism as it attempts to reproduce its values-driven operations in different cultural contexts?

Learning Objectives

The learning objectives developed for the Ben & Jerry's session were written to be general enough so that they could be adapted to a variety of corporate cases or scenarios that might have a similar context:

Leadership: Reflect on what leadership characteristics are necessary to successfully carry out a role of authority involving decision-making in an international company that is values-led.

Scalability: Determine whether the same values-led strategy for a small scoop shop in Vermont, United States, can be implemented in international operations.

Cultural Compatibility/Transferability: Understand the concept of sustainability and how it applies to international as well as domestic organizations.

Financial Stewardship: Wrestle with the concept of financial stewardship and decide if the concept should change for an organization whose stock is closely held versus one whose stock is widely dispersed.

Integrative Linkages/Sustainability: Analyze the activities in all the functional areas of an international organization and evaluate which activities are sustainable and which are not.

Decision-Making: Make recommendations for the future direction of the company.

Spontaneity/Creativity: Learn to respond to interview questions in valid and creative ways, with prior knowledge of only the nature of the questions to be asked.

Team Work: Work with other students in various aspects of the experience.

Some of these learning objectives were given a different emphasis in Calgary's program from those used in Henley's program, and the implementation process used to achieve these objectives (discussed later) was also adapted. However, the same set of learning objectives was used in both programs.

Preparation of Students for the Integrated Session (IS)

In order to marry successfully the practical experience with the theory, the integrated business experience needs to include two elements: (1) knowledge about the company itself; and (2) theoretical constructs that are appropriate for achievement of the learning objectives. The specific knowledge about the company, garnered through various databases, company communications, etc., must be researched by the students before the actual IS is held. Exchange of information can be facilitated by supplying students with some information on the company and direction as to where to find more. Theoretical constructs that apply to the learning objectives can be presented either before or after the IS itself. These two aspects were approached quite differently at the University of Calgary and the Henley Management College.

Knowledge About the Company Itself. At the University of Calgary, a deliberate attempt was made to use Ben & Jerry's Annual Report as a learning tool in the accounting instructional modules of the MBA program that occurred prior to the IS involving Ben & Jerry's. In addition, several weeks before the IS the students were provided with selected articles (Scott & Rothman, 1994), a case (Pearce & Robinson, 1997), Internet information, and a written analysis assignment that was to be handed in the day of the IS. The students were to answer the following questions:

> How should Ben & Jerry's balance responsibility to its share-holders with its commitment to social responsibility? Which takes precedent? Are they compatible? Give specific examples of what you would continue and what you would change. If you recommend change, suggest what you would do instead. Be sure to consider all parts of their mission statement.

Although students were directed to use any materials at their disposal, it was suggested that one of the frameworks useful for analysis could be the sustainability triad concept and that specific examples of Ben & Jerry's activities should be identified to represent the overlap among the social, economic, and ecological dimensions. The written case analysis required students to delve more thoroughly into the company's mission and to consider whether or not they agreed with the company's current direction. If so, why; and if not, why not.

At Henley, an alternative approach was taken for the students to get to know the company. As the program at Henley attracts students from all over Europe as well as the United Kingdom (UK) and has periods when the students are not at the College, the use of several distance learning techniques and technologies is essential. One of the technologies that is an integral part of Henley's program is the use of Lotus

Notes (a technically robust, groupware package) for both an e-mail environment for the students and for customized Notes applications to support information sharing and the syndicate-based group work necessary for preparation in the various learning modules the students are studying. Approximately a month before the actual IS was scheduled to occur, students were introduced to the activity via a custom Lotus Notes application, an interactive communication tool. They were guided through the issues with three sets of questions. To start the discussion process, the application was "seeded" with a number of selected documents from Ben & Jerry's (both corporate and UK-specific) websites and other Internet resources, and other printed article references via Lotus Notes relevant to the issues in the exercise and the company. They were then asked to explore on their own for more information, to discuss their findings among their group members, and then to post (share) their opinions to the Open Discussion via the Lotus Notes application.

The following questions were posed to the Henley students, roughly at two-week intervals:

What is Ben & Jerry's Homemade, Inc. all about?

Will Ben & Jerry's corporate culture work effectively for a variety of countries and cultures? How does the company handle the challenges of "going international?" What are the types of challenges they can expect (or may have already encountered)?

Will the company's approach to corporate social responsibility work effectively as a base for business development in other cultures? Do you think that their creative, somewhat off-the-wall" approach of combining fun and business will create good opportunities to work with non-profit organizations in other countries and cultures? Why or why not?

Theoretical Constructs. The knowledge about the subject company and its activities must be viewed in light of the theoretical constructs that are appropriate for achievement of the learning objectives. Again, this aspect of the experience was accomplished somewhat differently at the University of Calgary and Henley Management College. For Calgary, this integrated session was the last of a series of four IBEs, and for Henley it was the first.

At the University of Calgary there were several prior, functional modules in which core material was presented. Then, the students were to use their various knowledge sources, as well as some additional resources, in order to prepare some advanced assignments before the actual IBE. For example, previous IBEs gave the students approaches for addressing complex issues.

Furthermore, policy and strategy classes gave students several different frameworks for analyzing ethical dilemmas. The use of these frameworks attempts to ensure that students actually recognize, analyze, and decide courses of action rather than either ignoring the dilemma or rationalizing that the short term economic solution is best. Accounting classes used Ben & Jerry's Annual Report throughout the semester not only to understand the company's financial statements but also as a source for other valuable information about the company's operations. The company's Social Audit Report also provides access to information about the success of the company's social and environmental initiatives. The human resources classes provided a theoretical background for different philosophical viewpoints on whether for-profit organizations should be involved in charitable and social activities that appear to be only tangentially related to the core mission of the organization. Management information systems classes included discussions on managing outsourcing relationships, handling the legal and ethical aspects of information systems, selecting and managing relations with both suppliers and customers, and developing the relationships between technology and organizational strategy.

Although at Henley the students had over two months of functional area instruction (spread over the previous year of their program) in which they were given various analytical tools, the tools were generic and had not specifically been applied to a company using a values-led strategy. Rather than preparing the students with theoretical models that would apply to companies like Ben & Jerry's before the actual integrated session, the students were exposed to a panel composed of faculty members who addressed the following question directly after the integrated session:

> Why should the issues of corporate ethics, behaviour and values be relevant to every class member in this class?

Following the presentations by the faculty members, there was a question and answer session. Students were then sufficiently primed for some workshop-style, small group discussions to explore the potential strategies for Ben & Jerry's to enter the UK market and then Continental Europe. Following about 45 minutes of workshop discussions, each group reported in a plenary class session. The knowledge gained from this somewhat theoretical discussion (both process and content) is applied, in part, later in the program as part of each student's Integrated Strategy Project.

The Integrated Session (IS) Itself

Thus far, the discussion has been on the preparation or the follow-up associated with the integrated business experience (IBE). The integrated session (IS) itself occurred for both Calgary and Henley as a one-half day experience. The students were not told before the day of the IS exactly what the activities would be. When they came into the classroom on the day scheduled for the IS, they were given a schedule and directions for the day's activities. For this session, students were to work in teams. They were instructed that they were about to participate, in small groups, in three interview sessions, and they would play a different role in each one of the sessions.

For Calgary the three roles were CEO candidate; Morrie Baker (a Ben & Jerry's franchise owner located in Montreal, Quebec, Canada); and (together) Ben Cohen and Jerry Greenfield (founders of the company). Playing the role of the franchise owner required representing the interest of the scoop shop franchisees and in particular those from non-US countries.

For Henley, the three roles were adjusted to explore a real and current issue that the company was facing regarding its expansion in the UK. As the company planned to implement its social mission in the UK but wished to do so in a manner that would consider cultural differences, the candidate was being interviewed for the (fictitious) position of Charity Partnership Champion rather than the position of CEO. The person in this position was cast as in charge of "organizing and leading new and creative initiatives that would create and strengthen their partnerships with socially conscious, charitable organizations in the UK." The Chairperson of the Child Anti-Poverty Society (fictitious) was to represent "the general interests of charitable organizations which might be potential partners with Ben & Jerry's (UK)." This role replaced the franchisee in the Calgary experience. The founders of the company, and by definition the "value guardians," Ben Cohen and Jerry Greenfield, were important roles included in both experiences.

Certain characteristics of the interview process helped students to internalize the concepts related to business ethics and corporate responsibility: lack of knowledge of activity planned; a series of rapid-fire questions; and the necessity to play several different roles. Each of these is discussed briefly below:

- Lack of knowledge of the specific activity planned for the day of the IS required the students to think quickly (both the preparation session built into the day and the interview itself) without the advantage of advanced preparation for specific questions. In the debriefing, the issue of honesty in the candidate's answers was discussed, especially regarding values. It was observed that this process helped interviewers determine if the candidate was indeed true to his/her value set and those of the company through the consistency of answers, both direct and indirect.
- The series of rapid-fire questioning not only aided in determining the candidate's honesty, but it also gave the candidate a means of self-exploration and personal insight into exactly what values make up his/her value set and whether or not a values-led strategy is consistent with his/her own personal beliefs.
- The necessity of playing each of the roles helped the students understand the others' positions in wrestling with difficult issues of business ethics and corporate responsibility. This ability is crucial in helping to resolve difficult ethical dilemmas prevalent in many of today's international business situations.

Then, the students were the benefactors of a "real life" experience in corporate responsibility as they enjoyed taste-testing different flavours of Ben & Jerry's ice cream, yoghurt and sorbet that were sent especially for this session. In both the Calgary and Henley experiences, a company representative took part in the experience.

Evaluations and Feedback

Both institutions provided a means of feedback to the students for the interview process. As well, the students were given a means to comment on the total experience. In Calgary's experience, following the entire IBE, the faculty members did provide a graded assessment in line with the learning objectives that were set out previously for both the written assignment and the interview process. Henley's experience was not graded at the point of the IBE. However, as mentioned before, Henley students were to follow through both with a personal learning reflection exercise and in their Integrated Strategy Projects. For the Henley students those aspects are not completed until several months after the IBE.

Summary Framework

A framework (see Table 1) is provided to summarize certain program characteristics that the authors feel should be present in order for the IBE and the IS to be successful. The framework shows how the elements were then personalized to fit the unique characteristics of each of the Calgary and Henley programs. Certainly, two experiences do not allow sufficient generalizable evidence that these instructional techniques will work in other MBA programs. However, the experience has been adapted successfully to meet the needs of two quite different MBA programs in different countries. Therefore, these broad, general guidelines have been provided to help other institutions consider how they might adapt the experience to their own needs. In Table 1 items are italicized that are different in the two programs: Calgary and Henley.

Comments from Students and Faculty

Following the IBE and IS at each institution, the students and participating faculty members were asked for their comments and observations on the value of both the process and the content aspects. Although this particular feedback was not collected scientifically, both institutions felt it was necessary to determine whether it would be beneficial to continue the IBE and IS process, and if so, what aspects should be remain and what aspects should be changed. This qualitative information, along with other quantitative information (discussed earlier), was used to determine if the objectives were accomplished.

Student Reactions. Students were simply asked to comment on what they thought of the Ben & Jerry's IBE. They were given no prompts. Nor were they asked to comment specifically on its integrative nature, or the values-led approach, or the international setting. However, the

TABLE 1. General Guidelines for Program Adaptation

Program Characteristics	University of Calgary	Henley Management College
Program Mission	integration of functional areas; issues of corporate responsibility in an international setting.	integration of functional areas; issues of corporate responsibility in an international setting, *personal development.*
Learning Objectives	derived from mission, some were given more emphasis than others depending on the nature of the program	derived from mission, some were given more emphasis than others depending on the nature of the program
Program Structure (IBE)	*specific advanced preparation* through functional modules of both knowledge of company and theoretical models; *advanced case analysis written assignment;* interview process; debrief	*general advanced preparation* through functional modules; *specific advanced preparation of knowledge of company through Lotus Notes materials and discussion;* interview process; debrief; *faculty forum on values-led strategy and theoretical models discussion; debrief*
Subject Company	Ben & Jerry's Homemade, Inc., but other companies with a values-led approach were discussed which operate in either *Canada or the United States*	Ben & Jerry's Homemade, Inc., but other companies with a values-led approach were discussed which operate in the either *the United Kingdom or Europe*
Knowledge of Company	*provided through accounting module, selected library* and Internet resources, *and an advanced written case analysis assignment*	*provided through documents and discussion via Lotus Notes;* Internet resources; *additional materials were provided discussing the company's UK experience.*
Theoretical Models/ Constructs	*provided in functional modules prior to the integrated session (IS)*	*provided in a panel presentation and discussion after the integrated session (IS) and expected to be applied later through the Integrated Strategy Project*
Integrated Session (IS)– Interview Process	no prior knowledge of day's activities; series of rapid–fire questions in an interview process; required to play all three roles with different perspectives.	no prior knowledge of day's activities; series of rapid–fire questions in an interview process; required to play all three roles with different perspectives.

TABLE 1 (continued)

Program Characteristics	University of Calgary	Henley Management College
Roles–Interview Process	*CEO; franchise owner;* company founders – discussion of the *future direction* of the company in an international setting	Charity Partnership Champion; *charity representative;* company founders–discussion of a *current company strategic issue as it applies to the UK*
Assessment/Evaluation	both the written assignment and the interview process were *graded;* other peer–feedback mechanisms were provided	the interview process was *ungraded* but provided peer–feedback; *personal learning reflection experience required; learning to be incorporated in an Integrated Strategy Project that is graded at a later date*

comments suggest that the framework used was instrumental in accomplishing the two broad-based learning objectives that were set out for the IBE:

- understanding corporate responsibility or values-led strategy in an international business setting.
- integration of traditional functional disciplines (such as accounting, human resources, strategy, information systems, etc.)

As the students from the University of Calgary are given an entrepreneurial focus in their MBA in Enterprise Development, some of the comments from Calgary's students reflect this emphasis more than Henley's students. However, students from both the University of Calgary and Henley recognized the value of the integrative nature of the experience.

Novel, innovative and interactive day. Obviously, well thought through from the college end, and this is appreciated. (Henley)

The Ben & Jerry's session made me realize that it is important to look at a business from all different aspects. This skill is essential for an entrepreneur. (Calgary)

The CEO candidate and his group members had to familiarize themselves with the strengths and weaknesses of the operational, financial, human resource, and philanthropic activities of Ben & Jerry's. We then had to determine ways in which change could be made within these different activities as a means of improving the health of the company as an earnings generating firm while still preserving the company's unusually strong mandate of giving to the community. This was easier said than done. (Calgary)

Several students recognized the benefits from the experiential aspect of the process and felt that they were placed in a position of actually "wrestling" with the company's difficult decisions in attempting to internationalize its operations:

> The sessions helped to bring the company "to life," especially the strong Ben & Jerry's culture. One got a sense of what it would be like to work for this company through the role-playing sessions. (Calgary)

> The combination of Lotus Notes, role play, reflection, debate, a B&J representative and ice cream testing immersed you in the topic, making the issues more visible to the participant. (Henley)

> Good way to get a real up-to-date feel for the organisation. (Henley)

Other comments from the students reflected insight into the difficulties of balancing social, economic, and ecological interests in order to sustain the company. In some situations the role-playing helped to see the "other side" of an ethical dilemma more clearly. In other situations, the students realized how difficult it is to determine an individual's value set from an interview.

> When it is your own money on the line you can do as you please. However, once you have accessed the public capital markets then you have a new set of responsibilities, and your own agenda must be balanced with the shareholders' desires. However, a company can never please everyone. As a result, a company has to have a strong sense of its values; consequently, the business must be conducted according to these values. (Calgary)

> One question was especially difficult: I was asked whether I would allow a Montreal franchise to continue operating in Que-

bec if that province separated from the rest of Canada. My immediate response reflected only my personal values. This question quickly made me realize how complex it must be for a well-intentioned firm to decide on how best to react to a controversial event and do so in the best interest of the community, employees, shareholders, the company's social mandate, and the company's "bottom line." (Calgary)

Role play is difficult to simulate. I watched a lively candidate apply for a job with Ben and Jerry. His assessors were focused on destructive rather than constructive questioning. The challenge was to catch him out, perhaps more like an interview for a position as Tax Inspector Grade III. (Henley)

The questions I received challenged the views our group had formed and showed just how complex it must be for a profit-making firm to give to the community in a judicious way with finite resources. Some of the questions I needed to answer were: Whether or not Ben & Jerry's ice cream should be sold in Russia? Which community activities should continue if financial performance deteriorated? How much influence should a local franchisee have in developing a set of local community initiatives. (Calgary)

The B&J case study experience was a good forum for learning about a relatively new subject. The mixture of preparatory work then the various methods of approaching and dissecting the concepts meant one got a fuller understanding. It was a good way of introducing ethical business to a class mostly made up of cynics with a degree of testosterone poisoning as it showed them that, whatever the motives, it is possible to be conscientious and responsible and still make money which is still their driving "value." (Henley)

Some students commented on the effectiveness of the teaching/learning technique itself. Even though most students felt that the technique provided them a framework within which they could be creative, one student did see the experience as inhibiting creative thought.

I spent almost four years teaching adults and am always interested to see the techniques used to support learning. I must say I really enjoyed the session and found it of great benefit. I realized that after the third role play had gone so well for all participants that it was a reflection of the technique used which enabled us to understand the issues and refine our techniques for each subsequent role play. I also enjoyed the presentations which kept me both interested and "thinking."

Understanding the benefits of pursuing more than just pure profit in business is difficult for people in some sectors to accept. (Henley)

The experience provided basic knowledge for researching company. It gave greater insight into interview techniques; however, it inhibited free thoughts about the company and was rather prescriptive. I felt that I had to take them at face value which I still find difficult to do. Therefore innovative thought was stunted. (Henley)

I think ice-cream testing should be a mandatory part of this exercise. (Calgary)

Faculty Reactions. At both institutions, in general, the faculty felt that the session resulted in an engaging, wonderful learning teaching experience and provided a great opportunity to cross disciplines. Even though the IBE and the IS required considerable advanced preparation and co-ordination among faculty members, the IS itself resulted in little if any actual teaching but rather facilitation, guidance, and feedback on their part. The students themselves engaged in a self-directed, adult-learning experience within the guidelines provided by the faculty. The faculty felt that the exercise was successful in fulfilling the objectives set out for the IBE. The experience also provided faculty with an opportunity to think about how IBEs and ISs could be adapted to other themes or topics.

One member of the technical development team at Henley offered the following observation:

I know that management colleges are taking the "innovation" idea more seriously now (a friend of mine at INSEAD did a case study on my own "small company"). I really think that Henley could benefit more from techniques such as this B&J role playing exercise, which focuses on small companies. Next time, perhaps, we could place more emphasis on the innovation and creative aspects and how large companies can learn from the smaller ones.

IMPLICATIONS

The Ben & Jerry's IBE provided an opportunity to use current case materials in a highly integrative process that was fun yet provided a solid context of meaningful content for the students. Several characteristics of this experience addressed criticisms of current MBA programs and therefore help to prepare graduates for dealing effectively with complex, international organizational situations.

- The students were placed in the position of an existing international company and asked to help solve its ethical dilemmas; thus, making ethical decision-making more true to life.
- The active involvement of company personnel made the experience personalized for the class and actively demonstrated the potential value of the students' ideas and approaches for the company in dealing with a current (and real) situation.
- The experiential learning approach was grounded in theoretical constructs, presented either before or after the IS. This helped students to conceptualize how a practical application is explained by the theory.
- Faculty members collaborated explicitly in the session thereby re-enforcing the necessity of integrating disciplines.
- Creative approaches were encouraged in allowing use of any materials, frameworks, theories, or experiences the students could muster, suggesting more than one solution to addressing decisions.
- By using a real and current situation, provided by the company, as the basis for the exercise, the relationships and cooperation between the business schools and the company were strengthened.

The apparent success of this experience suggests that relevant and meaningful issues can be addressed in the classroom by developing stronger university-community alliances. Through these alliances, students learn by placing more emphasis on "actions" rather than "words." The students can also learn that there are different ways of doing business by "putting them on and trying them out" for a day. This type of session provides explicit evidence of the core values of an MBA program. It further illustrates that corporate challenges are never uni-dimensional, that students should have both knowledge and implementation capability, and that we need to recognize and thank those who help us achieve. Table 1 suggests general guidelines for program adaptation to other university MBA programs. The authors may also be contacted for further information.

CONCLUSION

The intent of the overall IBE module is to provide broad, integrative corporate issues for the MBA students to consider in an active-learning context. The specific objectives for the international corporate ethics session (using Ben & Jerry's as the case company) were to provide a good opportunity to understand and appreciate the full dimensions, interactions and implications of corporate ethical behaviors and sustainability of organizational health in an integrative fashion. The framework and techniques described in this paper appear to be adaptable to other programs, both graduate and undergraduate, as well as to other case companies in a similar context.

Indications from both faculty and students at both institutions show that the process was a meaningful learning exercise. It provided opportunities for creative learning, active involvement and engagement, vigorous exploration of the significant issues, and full recognition of the variety of ways to address the same issues. We fully intend to continue to include such sessions in the programs.

REFERENCES

Angel, James & Pietra Rivoli (Winter, 1997). Does Ethical Investing Impose a Cost Upon the Firm? *Journal of Investing* 6 (4) pp. 57-61.

Bloom, B.S. (1956). *Taxonomy of Educational Objectives: The Classification of Educational Goals.* New York: D. McCay.

Caux Round Table Principles for Business (1994). Caux Round Table (http://www.cauxroundtable.org).

Cochran, Philip L. & Robert A. Wood (1984). Corporate Social Responsibility and Financial Performance. *Academy of Management Journal* (27) 1 42-56.

Cohen, Ben & Jerry Greenfield (1997). *Ben & Jerry's Double-Dip.* Simon & Schuster: New York, New York.

Collins, J.C. & Porras, J.I. (1998). *Built to Last: Successful Habits for Visionary Companies.* Century Ltd. (Random House), London.

De Geus, Arie (1997) *The Living Company: Growth, Learning and Longevity in the Business World.* London: Nicholas Brealey Publishing.

Evans, Norman (1992). *Experiential Learning: Assessment and Accreditation.* New York: Routledge.

Falkenberg, Loren & Irene Herremans (1995). Ethical Behaviors in Organizations: Directed by the Formal or Informal Systems? *Journal of Business Ethics* 14, 133-143.

Gautschi, Frederick H. III & Thomas M. Jones (1998). Enhancing the Ability of Business Students to Recognize Ethical Issues: An Empirical Assessment of the Effectiveness of a Course in Business Ethics. *Journal of Business Ethics.* 17(2) January, 205-216.

Herremans, Irene M., Parporn Akathaporn & Morris McInnes. (1993). An Investigation of Corporate Social Responsibility Reputation and Economic Performance. *Accounting, Organizations and Society* (18)7/8 587-604.

Herremans, Irene M. & Michael E. Wright (1992). The International Accounting Education Needs of Employees of International Firms. *Journal of Teaching in International Business*, 3(4) 1-21.

Herremans, Irene M.& Michael E. Wright (1994). Global Trade is Blurring National Boundaries . . . Are Government Accountants Prepared? *Journal of International Accounting Auditing & Taxation* 3(2) 271-286.

Kuhn, James W. (1998). Emotion as Well as Reason: Getting Students Beyond "Interpersonal Accountability." *Journal of Business Ethics.* 17(3) February. 295-308.

Lazere, Cathy (1997). Ethically Challenged. *CFO: The Magazine for Senior Financial Executives.* 13(4) April. 40-41.

Mastrandonas, Andrew & Polly T. Strife (Fall & Winter, 1992). Lessons from Investors. *The Columbia Journal of World Business.* 234-240.

Menzel, Donald C. (1997). Teaching Ethics and Values in Public Administration: Are We Making A Difference? *Public Administration Review.* 57(3) May/June. 224-230.

Milne, Markus J. (1996). On Sustainability; the Environment and Management Accounting. *Management Accounting Research.* 7. 135-161.

Noreen, E. (1988). The Economics of Ethics: A New Perspective on Agency Theory. *Accounting, Organizations and Society.* 13(4) 359-369.

Novak, Joseph D. & D. Bob Gowin (1984). *Learning How to Learn.* New York: Cambridge University Press.

Pearce, John A. II & Richard B. Robinson, Jr. (1997). Ben & Jerry's Homemade, Inc.: "Yo! I'm Your CEO!" *Cases in Strategic Management* Fourth Edition. Chapter 8: pages 1-14. Richard D. Irwin.

Piper, Thomas. (1998). *Can Ethics Be Taught-Leadership, ethics, and corporate responsibility.* Efmd FORUM 98/2. European Forum for Management Development.

Scott, Mary & Howard Rothman (1994). Chapter 4: Ice Cream & Integrity. *Companies with a Conscience.* Carol Publishing Group. New York, New York.

Scott, R. Neil & Charles Smith (1992). Corporate Annual Reports and the Information Needs of Individual Investors. *Journal of Business & Finance Librarianship.* 1(3) 3-17.

Sturdivant, Frederick D., James L. Ginter & Alan G. Sawyer (1985). Managers' Conservatism and Corporate Performance. *Strategic Management Journal.* 6. 17-38.

Update (June, 1998). *Internal Auditor.* pp. 13-20.

Webster's New Universal Unabridged Dictionary, Deluxe Second Edition (1983). Simon & Schuster. USA.

White, B.J. (1980). Internal Control of Practices: Formality, Informality, and Effectiveness. In R.K. Mautz, W.G. Kell, M.W. Maher, A.G. Merten, R.R. Reilly, D.G. Serverance, & B.J. White. *Internal Control in US Corporations: The State of the Art.* Financial Executives Research Foundation: New York, New York. 337-344.

Wokutch, Richard E. & Barbara A. Spencer (1987). Corporate Saints and Sinners: The Effects of Philanthropic and Illegal Activity on Organizational Performance. *California Management Review.* XXIX(2) Winter. 63-77.

Index

Printed in the United States
by Baker & Taylor Publisher Services